GRAPES AND THE WIND

Las Uvas y el Viento
Pablo Neruda ©1954
Heirs of Pablo Neruda and Fundación Pablo Neruda ©1999
Translation: Michael Straus © 2017
Introductory essay: Dr. Helene Jf de Aguilar
Design: Practical People
Illustrations: Anna Pipes

Identifiers: LCCN 2017041423 | ISBN 9781944682989
Classification: LCC PQ8097.N4 A2 2018 | DDC 861/.62-- dc23
LC record available at https://lccn.loc.gov/2017041423

I left my country was published in *The Missouri Review* (May 2017), available online at:
missourireview.com/michael-straus-from-pablo-nerudas-grapes-and-the-wind-translation/

Flying to the sun and *The parade* were published in *Columbia:
A Journal of Literature and Art*, Issue 55 (Spring 2017).

Faraway, in the deserts was published in *Disonare* (July 2017), available online at:
disonare.tumblr.com/post/164807584592/el-quincenal-presents-nerudas-grapes-and-the-wind

Note on the Type: Set in Amster. Designed by Francisco Gálvez Pizarro

Pablo Neruda

GRAPES AND THE WIND

Translated by Michael Straus

Introductory Essay by Helene Jf de Aguilar, Ph.D.

TABLE OF CONTENTS

Introduction to the Poem

Pablo Neruda is by far the most widely known poet ever to emerge from Latin America and unquestionably one of the twentieth century's literary icons, a Nobel Prize winner with an output running to some 39 volumes. He was a diplomat, an avowed communist, a lover as well as a fighter, a tireless traveler. *Las Uvas y el Viento/ Grapes and the Wind*, published in 1954 but never until now translated into English, reflects this multiplicity of character throughout its 20+ chapters, written as they were over the course of Neruda's wanderings through Europe and Asia during a period of exile from Chile in the early 1950's.

Any Neruda reader knows that he is no respecter of Pascal's suggestion in the *Pensées* that mankind would be better off if people would just sit quietly in their rooms. He rarely inclines towards the silent, the still and the pallid. Even his expressed preference for travelling without leaving his native land and home (or what he calls "my own deepest self") refers to the Chile-forever-in-my-heart motif unmistakably recurrent throughout his poetry.

In its unflagging energy, its apotheosis of ravishing imagery, its passionate plunges into every secret of the physical world, its limitless flexibility and rhapsodic response to all stimuli, public and private, material and emotional, rational and mystic, its astounding and unstoppable enthusiasms, Neruda's work as a whole, like this volume in particular, occupies a unique place in the twentieth-century's poetic map. If excess distresses you, don't read him.

In his memoir *Confieso Que He Vivido/I Confess that I Have Lived*, Neruda states that *Grapes and the Wind* was perhaps his favorite book. Yet he also claims it to be his least understood. Both observations are at first glance surprising, given the immense popularity of other Neruda volumes and the relative obscurity of this one. On more careful consideration, however, the preference and the reservation make sense. For all their incomparable linguistic richness and imaginative range, other Neruda collections focus on a more or less isolable topic or specific stylistic purpose. The *Veinte Poemas de Amor/Twenty Love Poems* are indisputably love poems. *Residencia en la Tierra/Residence on the Earth* is an experiment in surrealist communication. *Alturas de Macchu Picchu/Heights of Macchu Picchu* transcends but never bypasses its declared subject: the holy Incan site atop the mountain remains, however transfigured, always before the reader's eyes.

By contrast, the very title of the current volume, *Grapes and the Wind*, suggests other possibilities. Just as grape vines proffer discrete bunches of fruit, each cluster separate from its fellows, so too the poet's opus can be organized into thematic clusters – the love verses read as love verses, the poems about lost friends as poems about lost friends, the paeans to Stalingrad or Poland or Czechoslovakia as inspired (and inspiring) declarations of communist solidarity. Yet this closed focus is not a necessary, nor necessarily an advisable, approach. Certainly it is an approach to which the wind blowing where it listeth (*pace* John 3:8) will pay no attention.

The wind that blows through these poems is indifferent to apparent distinctions in subject matter. On page after page of *Grapes and the Wind* we encounter a gorgeous jumble of the poet's tales and topics and techniques, all in service of a profoundly interconnected universe. The entire book concerns pilgrimage, hope, beauty and memory: meeting Neruda's demands concerning any of the four is not easy. The pilgrimage proves exhausting. The hope, especially in the world's current political and societal climate, is embittering – and more so, I suspect, for readers old enough to remember the period in question. The beauty is almost literally shocking – it frequently hurts. Memory may turn out for the reader (never, it seems, for the poet) to be a mixed blessing.

In that regard, variations on the theme of the verb "volver" are one of several leitmotifs recurring throughout *Grapes and the Wind* – this is precisely because "going back," even in memory or longing, provides both poet and reader a much needed moment of repose in the poem's long journey of relentless forward motion. It allows one to slow down. So in certain poems the poet describes an actual, physical return to Chile, his own epic *nostos*. More frequently, the returning is part of a metaphoric Eternal Return. In many poems the seasons reprise their age-old cycle and their respective glories "come back." Titles of individual sections of the poem commonly reflect the theme (such as *Homesickness and Return* or *The Siren Returns*). And Neruda is always chiding erring nations – France, England, Spain – urging their "return" to some earlier era of serenity and probity which presumably presaged the improbably utopian future to which he believes all things are headed.

Neruda's pilgrimage, along which we are invited as fellow-travelers (in multiple senses, given his political loyalties), begins with the opening poem and never comes to an end: the very last lines of the book are an exhortation to ongoing movement. (Think Tennyson's "Ulysses," or a lot of Walt Whitman). Neruda is always on the move, on foot or on horseback, in boats or in planes, through every conceivable landscape. Included among his ceaseless excursions, especially those in which he finds himself "borne back ceaselessly into the past," are many intensely private recollections of individuals, whether personal friends or figures of historical significance: Picasso, Ehremburg, Julius Fûcik, Paul Éluard, Henri Martin, Pushkin, inter alia. These intimate recollections serve as soft-glowing rest stops. They have an indoors feel, and the clear edges of Persian miniatures.

The central sojourn of the poem, on the other hand, involves open-air visits to whole populations. In some two hundred pages the poet traverses thousands of miles, not as the crow flies but criss-crossing along convoluted routes, reporting on the state-of-the-union all over the world. Whatever the devastation of the immediate past, Neruda sounds exuberant. Arriving in Russia and eastern Europe, not to mention Germany, France, Italy, Spain, Greece and many smaller countries, less than ten years after the end of World War II, he pays reverent homage to the suffering undergone by so many for so long while remaining immune to despair. Where Whitman – another master of the Unbounded – "shrivels," as he puts it, "at the thought of God / At Nature and its wonders, Time and/Space and Death," rallying only through the seemingly greater mystery of his own Soul, Neruda quivers before a human future so sparkling with spiritual, technological and educational promise as to ensure a new Eden. Thus one of the poems within the chapter on Germany, titled *Young Germans*, brings a cry of joy to the poet's lips:

> Oh wonder!
> here is new life,
> tree of light, hive,
> endless granary,
> peace and life,
> branch and branch,
> water and water,
> grape cluster with grape cluster,
> from vanquished scars
> to newly ripened dawn.

And I forgot the ruins,
the burnt stone's runes,
the fire's lesson.
I forgot the war,
I forgot the hate,
because I saw life.
Oh youth,
German youth,
your spring's new guardians,
strong frank youth of new Germany,
look to the East,
look to the vast union
of beloved Republics.
See too how from her ruins
a strong smile
dawns in Poland.
Giant China has shaken loose
her chains filled with blood
and is now our unbounded sister.

Few poets dare to hoist so much weight into a scant twenty-nine short and lyrical lines. The jubilant flow of language and the thrilling tone could well lead the reader to overlook, or at least uncritically accept, the huge quantity of stuff transpiring in a very short space. Conspicuous is Neruda's burgeoning Nature (complete, appropriately enough, with grapes) explicitly bound up with the harvest and faintly biblical in its peace-and-honey vocabulary. Here is spring, bringing rebirth. Along with a fixed set of instantly evocative terms repeatedly deployed through most of the poetry as basic structural elements – among them honey, stone, light, blood, peace, grain, water, star – there surfaces his classic and ever-startling loveliness of imagery, "the burnt stone's runes." Here is the apostrophe to one's Fellow Man, a poetic stratagem and political *topos* that characterizes *Grapes and the Wind*.

If Neruda "forgot" the war and the hatred a good deal faster than most people could – faster, in fact, than many might consider seemly – he finds full justification for that recovery in the spell-binding brotherhood of man he sees welling up everywhere before him, in Germany, in the Soviet Union, in Poland, in China. Indeed, his gaze and his impassioned endorsement of what he sees ahead flash at the speed of light in every direction; the reader is ordered not simply to think about all these nations but rather to engage instantly with their struggles, to *love* them. From China's farmlands to Poland's factories, from young children's songs to old women's souls, everything in these war-ravaged lands greets us suddenly suffused with the potential for bliss, and like a page in Dickens, everything is crowded with activity:

> At dawn in the village
> children and light welcome me.
> The peasants showed me all
> their conquered lands
> and the communal harvest,
> the granaries, the homes
> of the ancient owner.
> They showed me the place
> where poor mothers threw
> their daughters over a cliff,
> or sold them, not that long ago,
> oh! Not that long ago.
> Now it seems a bad dream.
> (from *Everything is so simple*)

> These – "what are their names?"
> From the old walls of your country the
> great-necked men of wicked sword ask
> "Who are they?"

And from her rotunda sugar-breasted
regal Paulina, naked and cold –
"Who are they?" she asks.
"We are the land," say the furrows.
"Today we exist," says the reaper.
"We are the people," sings the day.
(from *To Guttoso, from Italy*)

Here life waits.
I have seen life in Gdansk
replenishing itself.
Cars kissed me
with steel lips.
Water quivered.
I have seen cranes pass stately
like castles over the water,
cranes of maritime iron,
newly built.
I have seen a giant
scrap mass crushed
iron upon iron
beaten
give birth little by little
to the cranes' form,
and awake from the depths of death
the majestic blue of the shipyard.
(from *Peace building*)

Detailed depiction of an object historically overlooked is a hall-mark of Neruda's work. Instances of his interest in items that have been pretty much taken for granted by everyone else can be found throughout his work. The three volumes of *Odas Elementales/ Elemental Odes*, published between 1950 and 1955 – it is important to remember how crushingly prolific Neruda was – consist in large part of very precise and delightful descriptions of small, self-effacing miracles rarely immortalized by Art: the artichoke, the crab, the onion. But even in the absence of any intrinsic lyric attraction, even commonplace animals, vegetables and fruits do lend themselves to the whimsical. Steel-lipped cars and metal cranes at work building shipyards are another matter. They belong to the how-the-steel-was-forged literary realm associated with the most didactic aspects of socialist realism: poets outside that school would be hard-pressed to perceive their appeal.

Neruda's ability to endow such objects with the same artistic worth traditionally ascribed to sunsets, to mountain ranges or to wildflowers beside a babbling brook – to make them, in short, Beautiful – is unequalled. He is enraptured by Russian children "marching seven days on the / Transiberian Railway / to dream clear dreams of iron and harvests" (from *Transiberian*). In "Forward!" he revels in what the socialist peoples will bring forth, as though socialism were a second Genesis: "trees, canals, / rice, steel / grains, factories, / books, engines, / tractors and cattle." In images like "the high plains of metallic Mongolia" (from *Young Germans*) or "the factory that speaks to the sky / with smoke words" (from "My brother was there") or "Men of all / lands and seas, / look how / our steel daughter grows" (from *Polish song*) he binds together seamlessly the industrial and the pastoral.

That Neruda seeks to integrate into the purity of natural beauty the largely industrial artifacts of human society bears witness not to an incidental caprice but rather a spiritual conviction that is one consequence of his political fervor, at its pristine height during the years of this book's development. When Latin America's most distinguished nature poet – there is, unfortunately, no better term for a literary orientation deserving of one – comes to exhibit the same delight in a carbine engine that he used to experience in the snow-dusted pine forests – and to express both delights in similar language – the expansion must mean something serious. After all, even in *Grapes and the Wind* the unreconstructed Wordsworthian Neruda makes frequent appearances, describing himself in *When, Chile* explicitly as a creature untouched by technology: "There are men/half-fish, half-wind, / There are other men made of water. / I am of the soil."

Later on in the same sub-chapter, clearly in part a political apologia ("The Party made me dismount / and I became a man"), he writes "I am a river" and describes his political aspirations for his homeland without the slightest departure from nature imagery:

> Far from you
> I am but half-land, half-man,
> and today once again spring passes,
> I fill myself with your flowers,
> with your victory on my forehead,
> my roots remain in you.

But what Neruda actually seems to be attempting is a new Creation, not in the ordinary sense of artistic creativity but more literally, in the Creationist sense. When Vicente Huidobro wrote that poets enjoyed divine powers ("El poeta es un pequeño dios"), he might have been talking about his younger and monumental Chilean colleague.

Flowing through Neruda's landscape – almost literally, given the ubiquitous rivers, seas and other waterways that are basic components of nearly all his work – is a current of Intelligent Design. Despite History, with all its catastrophic injustices, its tragedies, its cruelties, selfishness and stupidity, there is Something shaping our as yet unrealized and grotesquely rough-hewn ends and *Neruda is on to it!* This explains his complete immunity to fear or doubt, emotions that are entirely absent from all areas of his work. Over and over again in *Grapes and the Wind* we are assured of future brotherhood, material well-being, intellectual advancement and societal liberation. But these things are not presented as optimistic dreams. They are not fantasies that may or may not be realized.

They are rather the unquestionable shape of things to come, predestined and inevitable. Unique among utopian visionaries of the period, Neruda's utopian vision is unclouded by anxiety. Neruda *knows*. He is marching on ahead where we are all bound to follow. Indeed, he writes at times as if the Intelligence behind the Design were in reality his own.

Twenty years after the publication of this book came the release of the poet's acclaimed memoir, *Confieso que He Vivido*. In this spirited confession we read that Neruda has "absolute faith in human destiny," by which he means something positive, and that absolutely nothing, not even the nuclear threat, will weaken his certainty. Writing in the early nineteen seventies he describes mankind's woes as a "blink" ("un parpadeo") in the scheme of things and promises that "definitive light" is on the way: "We will all understand one another. We will move forward together. And this hope is irrevocable." Really?

"Tomorrow is a highway broad and fair," proclaims Lee Hays' hymn to socialist solidarity sung so convincingly by Pete Seeger. By 1974, however, when Neruda's memoir appeared, unwavering confidence in a happy future ("and hate and fear will never travel there / But only those who learn the gentle way / Of brotherhood...") was definitely in short supply. By the close of the twentieth century the supposed Great Men who for the Left were supposed to usher in the transformative golden age – Mao and Stalin, for instance – no longer received, let alone deserved, mass veneration as mankind's blessed redeemers. And whatever our political beliefs, we are likely to flinch at the invocation of Korea as guardian of "the proud treasure / freedom, not only / your freedom, Korea / but all freedom, / everyone's, / mankind's freedom" (from *Your blood*).

Overtly political poetry is by its very nature a hard sell, as can also be the case with overly-blunt visual art: little can attain the power of Goya's *Disasters of War* or, of course, Picasso's *Guernica*. And this volume admittedly has some strained efforts in this regard:

I beg you,
England,
be truly English
again,
do you hear me?
Yes, be England –
not Chicago.

(from *The great love*)

It is therefore easy to see how a volume replete with improbable in-
vocations, bizarre petitions – England, after all, is not planning to
be Chicago any time soon – and formal apostrophes to failed states
might fail to enchant many readers. Odds are likewise against
widespread delight in poetry featuring psalms of praise to leaders
now known for brutality and corruption. Yet *Grapes and the Wind* is
hardly alone among Neruda's explicitly political works and despite
the clear gap, as a factual matter, between aspiration and reality, the
impact of poems consecrated to such problematic figures remains
intact. So what renders the intermittent absurdities and exagger-
ated pontifications poetic? Odd as it may appear, the answer, as is
often the case with this poet, is Nature.

In *The Four Loves* C.S. Lewis remarks that while he never
learned about the existence of a God of glory from Nature, still it
was Nature that "gave the word 'glory' a meaning for me. I still do
not know where else I could have found one. I do not see how the
'fear' of God could have ever meant to me anything but the lowest
prudential effort to be safe, if I had never seen certain ominous ra-
vines and unapproachable crags." Leaving aside for the moment the
fear of God – Neruda ignores religion and is, for better or for worse,
impervious to the fear of God, although not to awe – the same is
surely true of the Chilean poet. His familiarity with ominous ra-
vines and unapproachable crags is stressed in many poems, and the
reverence they inspire is as indisputable as it is worshipful.

The long nature passages in *Grapes and the Wind* that eschew any proselytizing, or which are marked at least by less strident sociological conviction, share the immediacy and breathtaking beauty of the landscapes they seek to capture in words. They transmit the glory of their source. Thus in the very first poem following the Prologue to the volume, *Only a man*, we read that:

> Treetops touched
> on high, trembling together
> while beneath, hidden in the dark selva,
> birds from the cold North
> quickly flying
> cry crossing –
> cold birds,
> foxes trailing lightning tails,
> a great leaf falling,
> my horse crushing
> the pale bed of a sleeping tree
> yet young trees
> still below the earth
> new trees
> know each other and touch.
> Deep beneath the ground
> one root
> one perfumed shoot
> one jungle.

Opening and continuing on through four irregular stanzas in an ecstasy of purely descriptive sensation, *Only a man* concludes in a grave, contemplative credo:

> I believe
> we won't meet in the heights
> nor that anything awaits us

beneath the soil –
but here, upon the earth,
we are together.
We are one upon the earth.

A great deal of Neruda's nature poetry wends its way towards some philosophic truth which, once grasped, turns out to have been all the while its hidden source. In this regard, too, Neruda seems to be in spiritual agreement with Lewis, who holds that one does not really learn philosophy from Nature because "Nature does not teach. A true philosophy may sometimes validate an experience of nature; an experience of nature cannot validate a philosophy." The experience of Nature is continually referenced in connection with Neruda's political theory, and the philosophic association arises not from thoughts that "lie too deep for tears" in Wordsworth's terms, but from the two principal ideas behind these closing lines.

The thoughts are obviously not new, nor need they be: Neruda himself professed solid skepticism in regard to artists' stubborn insistence on their own originality. First, life on earth – life as one more manifestation of the force of nature – is the only life we will ever have. Second, no life is completely unrelated to the lives of others, any more than a single peak can be independent of the mountain range engulfing it, or an inlet from the ocean free from all influence the tides exert over the open sea. These two observations lead to a kind of imperfect syllogism. In Nature every individual will die but no individual exists truly alone. Human beings exist in nature. Human beings therefore will die as individuals but will never truly live alone. This is most famously John Donne territory insofar as Donne requires recognition of mankind's family bonds. For Neruda, the recognition is insufficient. Not living alone means living within a social order. And a social order entails social awareness, judgment, action and responsibility. In other words, it means obligatory engagement with politics. But how does this become *poetic*?

Many critics have noted the theme of union in Neruda's poetry, emphasizing its centrality in works of direct political tenor. In her astute preface to Delbolsillo's Spanish edition of *Las Uvas y el Viento* (Buenos Aires, 2003), Lucrecia Romera couples "la unidad" with the mythic dimension in which Neruda's aesthetic finds its origin and its fulfillment. It is this overarching framework of myth, reminiscent of the earlier-cited "treetops on high, touching each other," that makes feasible the fusion of three worlds Romera identifies as crucial to the book's structure and effectiveness: "the modern world of factories and steel, the historical world of revolutions, and the original world of grapes and wind and Earth" (my translation).

The evocative power of these entwined three "worlds" simultaneously channeled by a poet of Neruda's brilliance gives independent splendor even to his short-sighted or ill-advised political endorsements. The myth absorbs and transforms the negative, suspending disbelief. The myth supersedes the man. This is to say that for Neruda, the "real" Stalin of the present-day yields place to an idealized Stalin – the Hero, the Leader, the Emancipator. Mao was no doubt a deeply-flawed Prometheus, but a Prometheus nonetheless when viewed within a poetic framework meant to endure when the man himself is gone. What matters is the Ideal. Neruda adheres to an established tradition among historians. He is doing, something like what Constantine's biographer Eusebius did: presenting the emperor *as he should have been*, as a Model for future incarnations of power and progress.

That is why even his most blatantly propagandistic compositions, writings consecrated to deeply flawed and compromised men, need not be read as foolish apologetics. Neruda's paeans to fallen idols can yield to a yearning for what might have been. *On his death*, for example, is part of a very long section within the poem about Stalin, adulatory beyond belief – if taken at temporal face value. It thus begins with all creation reeling at the terrible news:

> Comrade Stalin, I was by the sea on Isla Negra,
> resting from battles and travels,

> when word of your death arrived like an ocean's blow.

Right from the outset the reader bears witness to the modern realm ("battles and travels"), the realm of revolution ("Comrade Stalin") and the natural realm ("an ocean's blow") combined with a vengeance.

Subsequent imagery confirms the tripartite status of our understanding and expands Neruda's attempt to rely on mythic truths, elaborating further the effects of a loss portrayed as cosmic:

> First there was silence, the stupor of things, and then
> it crashed from the sea like a great wave.
> Of seaweed, metals and men, stones, foam and tears
> was this wave made.
> From history, time and space the wave
> gathered his substance
> and rose, crying above the world
> until it came before me to beat against my shore
> and its mournful message threw down my doors
> with a great cry
> as if of a sudden the Earth broke apart.

These are luscious, opulent lines, fully imbued with the sweeping movement, the sense of transcendence and the complexity of association that mark Neruda's best work. They remind us, too, of just how Earthbound (the upper case is deliberate) a poet he is.

Not for nothing did he name three distinct collections (1933, 1935, 1947) *Residencia en la Tierra/Residence on Earth*. But *On his death* is an obituary. As such it requires an inventory of the deceased's times and accomplishments. Inventories in turn mean lists. There are numerous sorts of lists but in different ways they all allow ample scope for Neruda's incomparable dexterity with metaphor:

It was in 1914.
The rich men of the new century
sliced shares with their teeth from oil and islands,
copper and canals.
No flag lifted its colors
without splashings of blood.
From Hong Kong to Chicago the police
sought documents and tried out
their machine guns on the people's flesh.

Just what Neruda had against Chicago we will never know – the city shows up consistently on the wrong side of the struggle – but rich men using their teeth to slice market shares out of nature is perfectly clear.

It is a savage and bitter vision, akin to García Lorca's sighting of sleepless souls at sunrise in New York, just awakened to a new day and staggering along the streets "as if just emerging from a shipwreck of blood" (from *La aurora*, in *Poeta en Nueva York*, 1940). Other, and equally bleak, expressionist images slash through the grief of this eulogy: "A blood rain fell from the planet, / staining the stars." "War had stiffened the roads." Relief is provided at intervals by recurrent surges of an elemental beauty indifferent to human intentions even when due to human intervention. Responsive to Stalin's will "The deserts sang / for the first time with the voice of water."

At once the master of praise and the sometime victim of his own fervor, Neruda does occasionally stumble. To be sure, there are moments in which his attitude towards the Soviet wonder-worker is worshipful to the brink of hilarity. The assertion, for instance, that "Stalin is midday / the maturity of mankind and the people" wavers between the odd and the creepy; and certain evidence of godlike status seems silly:

He taught all
to grow, to grow,
plants and metals,
creatures and rivers
he taught them all to grow,
to yield fruit and fire.

The poem's last image of this second Creator places him in a scene amounting to a parody of blended Bible tales. Thus Stalin appears like a revised Moses, receiving a visit from the Holy Ghost, now in the guise of an oppressed flower:

In his last days the dove, Peace,
the wandering persecuted rose
alit on Stalin's shoulders, and the giant
lifted it to his forehead's height.
So the peoples saw peace.

It is unfortunate that this sort of tonal (and verbal) lapse leads to many critics' and many readers' too-casual dismissal of Neruda's political poetry if not, indeed, his political convictions. Such missteps should rather be celebrated: they are proof of human fallibility in a poet gifted with quasi-supernatural powers. Neruda calls to mind the purple bird described by Wallace Stevens as needing, despite – or more correctly, because of – the splendor of his plumage, "notes for his comfort that he may sing / through the gross tedium of being rare." His reckless rants cause no serious damage. They are merely cathartic.

Towards the conclusion of the poem anguish and agitation subside, to be replaced by precisely the unyielding, quiet courage demanded of good socialists. Alone on the beach – think Mathew Arnold – contemplating the nearly incomprehensible news of Stalin's death, Neruda will rally to the future. His tone changes.

His diction is suddenly subdued, stripped of myth, mysticism and literary devices.

> Facing the sea on Isla Negra I spied
> at half-mast Chile's flag in the dawn.
> The coast was lonely
> and a silver cloud was mixed
> with the ocean's solemn foam.
> In the midst of its mast, in its blue field,
> my homeland's single star
> seemed a tear between sky and land.

The simplicity of such verses stands in fierce juxtaposition to every aspect of the poet's more characteristic language, dissipating all violent emotion and facilitating by its unprecedented calm the reader's resignation to bereavement, to a transformed world: the first step towards renewed hope. There will *always* be hope. That is one constant of Neruda's messages. Another is our shared human-ity, attested to with great dignity and serenity in a conclusion that could almost be taken for prose, with the arrival at the poet's side of a fellow mourner, happily not another internationally renowned artist but a figure reassuringly representative of the common man:

> "But Malenkov will now carry on his work,"
> continued the poor worn-jacketed fisherman
> lifting himself up.
> I looked at him surprised thinking:
> How, how does he know that?
> Where did he learn it, on this solitary coast?
> Then I understood the sea had taught him.
> And so we mourned together, a poet,
> a fisherman and the sea
> to the distant Captain who on entering death
> left to all people, as a heritage, his life.

For the politically engaged, it turns out, sadness may tarry for the night but joy cometh in the morning.

These stanzas are full of a tenderness atypical of Pablo Neruda, whose voice, even in crushing emotional circumstances, inclines to the Splendid, the Overpowering and the Dazzling. Gentle passages do occur in his love lyrics, but they are not protracted. Quiet reflection lies as a rule outside his comfort zone, quickly yielding place to the undomesticated, surging intensity of perception and response that constitute his more natural habitat even in matters of the heart. *Grapes and the Wind* is deeply enriched, as earlier noted, by memories of visits – often, at least by implication, farewell visits – with people, alive or dead, who are personally dear to poet.

Since the subjects are public figures their significance can never be wholly divorced from their public roles as artists, as thinkers, or as shining lights illuminating mankind's collective future. As such, the moments Neruda allots to reflections on their purely personal significance – on what these individuals meant *just to him* – are strictly limited. Their sense of *privacy* comes as a shock. They are characterized by a Quaker-like plain speech, something one might call an "indoors" voice, too unlike his customary mode of expression to be missed, or for that matter, long sustained. The scarcity of such a tone imbues the stripped, unadorned grief to which it attests:

> I've just learned
> of Paul Éluard's death.
> Here, in the small envelope
> of a telegram.
> I closed my eyes, it was
> his death, some letters,
> and a great white void.
>
> (from *Paul's death came*)

Note that the eyes Neruda must close in order to process his friend's death are the same eyes that, wide open, elsewhere manage defiantly to survey cities crumbled into ruins, populations slaughtered and civilizations brutally dismantled, all the while hailing the redemption to come. Intertwining vines of complex imagery create a verbal rainforest in "The belt from Orinoco." Neruda wears, in this beautiful poem, "a river at my waist, / nuptial birds who in their flight lift / petals from the thicket." Estuaries and peaks and islands and a "green crocodile river" are soon added. By the end of the poem the populace is once again uniting to sing about freedom. Yet what sets all this in motion are the two first lines, absolutely intimate and absolutely straightforward: "Carlos Augusto sent me a leather belt/ from Orinoco." Another piece of homely clothing introduces *Here comes Nazim Hikmet*, setting in motion an analogous complexity of intricate rhetorical devices:

> Nazim, newly freed
> from prison, he gave me his shirt
> embroidered
> with golden threads,
> red like his poetry.
> Threads of Turkish blood
> are his verses.

Linked poems are not uncommon in *Grapes and the Wind*. *Arrival at Picasso's door* is the first of two reverent tributes to painters Neruda loved. Here too the opening line is as prosaic as is humanly possible: "I came to Picasso at six in the morning," a statement from which nobody would guess the subsequent thematic development ablaze with color and threat, nor the violence of the visual component to follow:

I also found the black cockerel of
encephalitic foam, with a branch of wire
and slums,
the blue cat with its toenail fan,
the tiger creeping above the skeletons.

The *ordinariness* marking the initial lines of these poems –
the innocuous simplicity of the information they convey – functions
like the unadorned and undramatic outer panels of a medieval trip-
tych which, when opened, stuns the viewer.

Longer interconnected series include the *Prague
Conversation*. Here nine close-linked poems evoke with majestic
pomp and solemnity ("Radiant Julius – from the honeycomb of
lives / cell iron and sweet, made of honey and fire!- / give us this
day as our daily bread / your essence, your presence") the life and
times of Julius Fûcik, yet the man himself, the *friend* Neruda wants
to immortalize, is presented in the very first lines, with the utmost
humility. So self-effacing is this hero, in fact, that he is not even present:

On Prague's streets each winter's day
I passed the walls of the stone house
where they tortured Julius Fucik.
The house says nothing, stone the color
of winter, bars of iron, deaf windows.

What could be less dramatic, or more *usual*, than to pass by a friend's
empty house and to remember him when nothing else does?

Within the chapter titled *The Last Goatherd* four splendid
poems are devoted to the doomed Spanish poet Miguel Hernández,
who only appears on the scene in the last one. The section as a whole
deals with the aftermath of the Spanish Civil War, a subject never
far from Neruda's consciousness. Its horrors occupy a special and
irreducible space in his heart. Since the Spanish fascists have won,

and unquestionably hold absolute power, optimism is obviously not sustainable. Nor is it possible for him to look back stoically on the conflict, upheld by the Promise so fundamental to his views on History, because the evil does not lie behind us as do the Nazis, the Tzars, the "masters, lords and rulers of all lands," to quote Edwin Markham. No liberating Stalin looms on the Iberian horizon.

The courageous patience with which Neruda is able to regard other devastations, and which he urges upon the reader in many poems, here fails him. That is why *Return, Spain*, the prologue to the Hernández chapter, emerges written entirely in a tormented frenzy of italics and suffused with expressionist sound and fury: *"Spain, you are haughtier than a festal day, / than a prophecy, than torture, / and the cruel tower of your lost voice matters not, but only hard / resistance, the stone that sustains."* The outrage and agony are nobody's secret and therefore become everyone's patrimony. The very universality of these sentiments renders them paradoxically impersonal. "If I should tell you," the first of the three poems thus savagely introduced, abandons rage along with its feverish italics in favor of a sorrow and regret similarly appropriate to Everyman when forced to face a ruin now past redress. Inner collapse reigns. The passion of the prologue is spent; there is nothing left to hold onto: "No, I have no keepsakes," says Neruda, speaking in a kind of class action for all those similarly situated. (He sounds, as it happens, exactly like his tremendous contemporary, Luis Cernuda, who having survived the Spanish Civil War, remarks in one of his numerous bitter poems on the subject, "Spain? A name. Spain is dead").

Nothing remains for Neruda but to brood, in stunning imagery, over the lost motherland – Latin Americans routinely refer to Spain as "la madre patria." He knows precisely what has been obliterated: "Granada red and firm, / black topaz, Spain / my love, hipbone / and skeleton of the world." But from its opening lines the next poem, "Our brother will arrive" starts to mitigate, if not transcend, despair. Where all seemed dead and finished – Spain was bone and skeleton – now "Something is happening, / fermenting, tears / moons, pains, sorrows." It is irrelevant that the "something" happening is not gleeful, because life is renewing itself:

> There is an ocean,
> a vast electric wind
> forming lightning bolts,
> something growing in your womb,
> Spain.
> We recognize
> the brother who comes.

By the close of *Our brother will arrive*, Neruda is on his metaphoric feet again. He summons the prostrate, defeated nation to recover itself, to fight back:

> Let your victory enter,
> open the doors,
> let your son open the door
> with stout red miner's hands,
> that the door of Spain may open,
> because this is the victory
> we lack
> and without that victory
> there is no honor in the land.

It is clear that "our brother" and Spain's new "son" are one and the same and that both arrive riddled, literally, with the past:

> give all your bones,
> the bones that don't forget,
> give him the open sockets
> of our bullet-riddled men,
> give him your life and mine.

It is also clear that Neruda expects the brother and son to save their homeland and be saved by her in turn.

What is not obvious, and will only become so in the last in the series of four poems in *The Last Goatherd* chapter, is that the son and the brother are to be the reincarnation, via wishful thinking, of Miguel Hernández, dead and buried since 1942. Hernández grew up in the countryside, herding goats. Introspective and guarded in his output – the dazzling, daring raptures of Neruda are alien to his poetic voice –Hernández rose from peasant stock against great odds – poverty, class prejudice and implacable family opposition – overcoming but never completely escaping this background. Like Neruda, he loved nature and derived from it much of his somewhat austere aesthetic vision; the countryside was his childhood home, and few childhood homes consist of unmitigated joy. His best work attests to his faithfulness in love; and it was his passionate commitment to the Republican struggle against Francisco Franco that led to his arrest. Incarceration, torture, sheer physical exhaustion resulting in terminal illness led to his death in prison, and he has served ever since as emblematic of martyrdom under the Franco uprising. Neruda's grief over Miguel Hernández finds initial expression in just the kind of uncomplicated introduction seen in the other poems addressed primarily to intimate remembrance or loss. The opening lines could not be more unadorned:

> His name was Miguel.
> He was a young
> goatherd by the outskirts
> of Orijuela. I loved him.

From this modest beginning emerges a work of convoluted, baroque expression. *The Last Goatherd* is a poem at once pastoral, elegy, eulogy and a call to combat. In the rapid and heart-stopping mood swings of its six pages we encounter, besides the intermittent prosaic checks along the way (e.g., "Miguel Hernández,/your land and people/ will live again in you," and later on "No one, Miguel, has forgotten you") all the poetic strategies that identify the Chilean master's output.

Metaphor and simile grow rampant, some luxuriant and some cozy, among other forms of imagery so peculiar to Neruda that they leap the boundaries of all official terminology. The Sublime beckons us through the ravishing perfection of the natural world, distinct from, yet ever bound to, mankind's worthiest endeavors. The unity of the individual with the People- a union sometimes portrayed as a conscious act of political will and other times as mystic and existential, a result of mankind's shared origin and end – emerges over and over again as a redemptive truth. Hope is the light that shines in the darkness of Spain's tragedy, and by extension, of all our conjoined tragedies:

> He was a fortress
> of songs and thunder,
> he was like a baker:
> with his hands he crafted
> his sonnets.
> All his poetry
> is like porous soil,
> drinking the rain –
> grains, sand,
> mud and wind –
> and it has the form
> of a Levantine vase,
> filled to the brim,
> of a queen bee's belly,
> it has the scent
> of clover in the rain,
> of amaranth ash,

of dung smoke, late,
upon the hills.
His poetry is corn gathered
in golden cluster,
a vineyard of black grapes, a bottle
of dazzling crystal
filled with wine and water, night and day,
it is a scarlet branch,
the Morning Star,
hammer and sickle written with diamonds
in the shadow of Spain.

The stanza resembles a glorious seizure. It provides an excellent compendium of all that stamps Neruda's work as his own - right down to the occasional jarring oddity, like the perplexing notion of the Communists' sign of proletarian brotherhood "written with diamonds." It is an orgy of sensory overload that leaves the reader ecstatically reeling, the predominant side effect of his poetic ethos. (That this deluge of imagery with all its whirling, diverse range of focus is ascribed to Hernández, a poet rather given to severe restraint, when it is so unmistakably characteristic of Neruda, is something of a conundrum). The world is almost too much with us here and yet, in spite of the frenzied cascade of descriptive free association, not one single verse could be deleted without weakening the effect of the whole.

Tucked into the whirlwind is even a brilliant stroke of Nerudan shorthand: what is "a Levantine vase," after all, if not a Grecian urn? The reference to Keats makes surprising sense in the context, for two reasons at the least. First, Neruda's entire opus is a vast liturgy for the worship of Beauty and Truth. Second, and more slyly, the allusion suits Hernández' hard-won familiarity with, and deep respect for, the master poets of the past. Neruda pays an artist's dearest tribute to his lost friend and admirer by setting him in the company of those who (*pace* Daniel) "shine like the firmament."

A stanza, in short, that appears to be in serious need of editing proves, upon analysis, not in the slightest condensable.

All poems are not created equal, and any poet as prolific as Neruda must expect a smudge of inconsistency in the quality of his or her work. A "bad" poem – one wholly lacking in verbal brilliance or imaginative vision – is certainly hard to find anywhere in Neruda's output, but *Grapes and the Wind* does provide, in a strangely endearing manner, instances of such sporadic weaknesses as do, rarely, undermine a line or a stanza. Indomitable courage can read like bravado. Elements of the imagery so insistently drawn from nature and so often presented as a source of wonder can become wearing: there are "stones" all over the place. The implacable political declamation that a priori alienates some readers is, of course, not in itself a defect, any more than a poem about a rabbit would be a bad poem just because some people have no interest in bunnies.

But the declamatory tone sometimes bears a slightly pro forma quality, as if it were carry-on luggage from a previous trip. Neruda's fantastic voyage in this volume entails so many stops and layovers that the hint of jet-lag creeping into a verse here or there is practically inescapable. Some messages and some metaphors suffer the fatigue that afflicts even the most indefatigable traveler. Unwieldy ones surface, and yet even when an overly ambitious image backfires, one is forced to admire the fearlessness of the poet's intent. The book stands as a full testament to the poet's genius. Its thematic range is complete. Its perfections and its imperfections represent the poet with uncanny accuracy.

Las Uvas y el Viento has been available in the original Spanish for nearly 60 years, but it has never been the first choice among Neruda readers, whether beginners or advanced. The early love sonnets and the 1950 *Canto General/General Song* figure as the most popular points of departure for neophytes embarking on the adventure. The *Residencias* and the *Odas Elementales* are favorites among readers of sophisticated literary taste. "Explico algunas cosas/I

Explain Some Things," one of the most acclaimed of all his poems, as heartbreaking as it is exquisite, appears in the extremely accessible 1937 *España en el Corazón/Spain in the Heart*. For a number of readers, in fact, this poem IS Neruda.

Yet whether as an introduction to or recapitulation of the poet's most profound attitudes towards life, the world and poetry itself, *Grapes and the Wind* is an excellent choice. Reading it as an introduction to Neruda may be rather a baptism by fire, but it is at the very least a rite of impeccable authenticity and a life-enriching experience. The poet himself warns us at the close of *The years grow* that we shouldn't expect to relax any time soon:

> I travel from one land to another
> testifying,
> summing up the ineffable,
> adding the steps,
> connecting the syllables
> of the song of the wind upon the earth.

Las Uvas y el Viento is neither restful nor soothing, but it is definitely a text for all seasons.

Helene Jf de Aguilar, Ph.D.

Pablo Neruda

GRAPES AND THE WIND

Prologue

Listen to me!

I went singing
wandering
between the grapes
of Europe
and beneath the wind,
the Asian wind.

Collecting the best
of those I met,
earthly sweetness,
pure peace,
and so I roamed and
wandered.

First to the finest of one land
then another

I lifted my voice with song
freedom found in the wind,
peace among grape vines.

Some men seemed
enemies to one another,
but taking shelter under the same
night sky,
they awoke
under the world's single light.

I entered their homes
as they dined,
home from their factories,
some laughing some crying.

They were all equals.

All their eyes
faced the light,
seeking true paths.

Together they sang
with one song
heralding the spring.

All of them.

And that's why I searched
wandering among grape vines
beneath the wind
seeking the best.

Now hear what I say.

I

THE GRAPES OF EUROPE

1

Only a man

I passed
through sharp-faced
Andean ranges
on horseback
among the trees.
The moss left
on the ground
its blanket
woven of a thousand years.
Treetops touched
on high, trembling together
while beneath,
hidden in the dark selva,
birds from the cold North

quickly flying
cry crossing –
cold birds,
foxes trailing lightning tails,
a great leaf falling,
my horse crushing
the pale bed of a sleeping tree,
yet young trees
still below the earth
new trees
know each other and touch.
Deep beneath the ground
one root
one perfumed shoot
one jungle.

Thorns claw me as I go,
hard stones piercing
my mount's hooves,
ice catching my heart
beneath torn clothes
with song and sleep.
Rivers born
beyond my ken drop swiftly,
seeking my life –
but a tree barred the road
as if it had begun to walk
and the jungle toppled it.
There it was
fierce as a thousand men,
hair streaming
swarming with insects,
rotted by the rain,
but I wished to keep myself
from death.

I leapt over the tree,
crushed it with an axe,
caressed its leaves lovely like hands,
held powerful roots
that knew the soil
much better than I.
I passed over the tree,
crossed all rivers,
foam carried me,
stones deceived me,
minute by minute
the green air forming
jewels
attacked my face,
burned my lashes.
And so I crossed the high cordillera
not alone
but with another man.
The trees didn't come,
surging water
that would have killed
did not come with me,
nor the thorn-filled ground.
Only a man,
a man alone was with me.
No help from the tree's hands,
lovely as faces,
nor the deep roots that know the soil.
Just him.
I don't know his name
but he was poor like me, had
eyes like mine, and with them

he found the path
for the next to pass.
And so here I am.
And therefore I am.

I don't believe
we will meet in the heights
nor that anything awaits us
beneath the ground –
but here, upon the soil,
we are together.
We are one upon the land.

2

The river

I entered Florence at night time
trembling
half asleep listening
to what the sweet river
sang to me. I don't know
what paintings or books say
(well, not all paintings or all books,
just some)
but I know what
all rivers say.
They speak the same language I do.
In wild lands
the Orinoco speaks to me
and I understand,

I understand histories I cannot repeat.
The river bears away my secrets
and what it asked me, that will I do,
little by little on Earth.
I recognized old words in the voice
of the Arno old words and
they sought their voice in me,
as one who never knew honey
and finding it learns its pleasures.
So I heard the voices
from Florence's river,
as if they had told me something
before I even came to be,
something only now heard:
dreams and travels joined me
to the river's voice,
lives on the march,
the blows of light bursting into history,
tercets ablaze like lamps.
Bread and blood sang to me
in the water's night time voice.

3

The City

And when in the Old Palace,
beautiful as a stone aloe tree,
I climbed the worn steps,
crossed the ancient rooms,
a worker

came out to receive me,
chief of the city, of the old river,
of the houses cut as from moonstone,
but I wasn't surprised:
the people's glory governed.
And I saw just past him
the tapestry's dazzling threads,
the painting that emerged
from twisted streets to show forth
beauty's flower
in all the world's byways.
The infinite rolling waters
of Florence's thin poet,
always cascading
never ceasing
his syllables forged
in red fire tempered in green water –
all this I spied behind his laborer head.
But it wasn't the halo of past splendor
that hid behind him:
it was the simplicity of the present.
As a man who
from loom or plow,
or factory dark
had climbed the terraces
with his people
there he was in the Old Palace,
without silk and without sword,
he who crossed with me the far cold
of the Andean range.
And immediately
beyond his head
I saw the snow,
the great trees that joined

on the summit and here,
newly upon the land,
he received me with a smile
and gave me his hand,
the same hand that showed me the path
there far away where I conquered
the hostile iron ranges.
And here it was no miraculous stone
that made me a citizen,
no procreative light,
not the painting's blue kindness,
not all the river voices
in that old silver stone city,
but a worker, a man,
like all men.

Therefore I put my faith in mankind
each night each day,
and when thirsty I trust in water,
because I have faith in mankind.
I believe that together we shall climb
the last stair-step
and from there see
truth shared,
simplicity planted in the soil,
bread and wine for all.

4

Diverting the River

In Romania's summer
I went toward the sea,
the pines steel green,
and by the sea I found a flowing river:

Romania's yellow Danube.

Mankind opened the slumbering
river bed, changed its course,
propelled it forward,
attacking with violent hands
hollowing out the soil
dynamite lifting
a branch of violet colored smoke.
The river's waist trembled
and it flowed,
running through other lands,
compelled,
fertilizing dry sands,
giving birth to fruit and wheat.

The river resisted
but mankind drove it forward,
whipped its haunches,
beat its foam,
tamed it and prevailed,
and across the sea the river flowed
and with it life.

I saw boys spotted
with dust and sweat, little ones
before the hostile and sterile ground,
proud and small,
opening the river's path,
showing me the central
future of its power, when
the water might give light
to those black regions.
I saw them, I touched them. I believe
that the great gods of long ago
seemed like the smiling children
who straightened
the river's yellow course
that tomorrow may dawn on
the land's new grapes.

5

Fruit

Sweet green olives of Frascati,
fresh as young nipples,
fresh as ocean drops,
distilled, earthly essence!

From the old soil
scratched with song,
renewed each spring
with the same mortar as people,

with the same substance as
that of our eternity, perishing
and being born, repeated
and new, olive groves
of the dry lands of Italy,
from the generous womb
in pain
continues giving birth to delight.
That day the olive,
new wine,
my friend's song,
my love at a distance,
dampened ground,
all so simple,
so eternal
like a grain of wheat,
there in Frascati
the walls punctured
by death,
war's eyes in the windows,
but peace received me
like the taste of oil and wine,
while all was simple like the people
who delivered me
their green treasure:
small olives,
fresh, pure flavor,
a delightful measure,
the blue day's breast,
earthly love.

6

The Bridges

Prague's new bridges, you were born
in the old city, rose and ash,
so the new man
might cross the river.
A thousand years wore out the eyes
of the stone gods
who from the old Karl Bridge
have seen comings and goings
old lives never returning
old lives –
from Malá Strana toward Moravia
feet find their paths, time's heavy trod,
the strides of the old Jewish cemetery
beneath twenty layers of time and dust
they pass and dance above the bridge,
while smoke colored waters
run toward ancient stone.

Moldava, little by little
you made yourself a statue,
grey statue of a dead river
with its old iron crown in front,
but now the winds
of history shake
your feet and your knees
and you sing, river, and you dance,
and you walk with new life.
It's different now with power plants.

The forgotten portrait
of the people smiles in their windows
greeting me.
Here now stand
the new bridges:
clarity filling them
courage calls
and says: "People, march forth,
toward future years,
toward wheat lands,
toward the mine's black treasure
shared among all."
And the river flows
beneath the new bridges
singing with history –
pure words
that will fill the Earth.

No longer do invaders' feet cross
the new bridges, nor the cruel carriages
of hate and war:
but now pass children's small feet,
the workers' firm feet.
And above the new bridges
you pass, oh spring,
with your bread basket and fresh dress,
while mankind, water, wind
dawn singing.

7

Picasso

In Vallauris each house
holds a prisoner.
It is always the same one.
It is smoke.
At times white-eyebrowed
fathers guard him,
oat-colored girls.
When you pass by
you see the smoke-guardians
sleep
and through the roofs,
between broken pots,
a blue conversation
between Heaven and smoke.
But there where fire
freely works
and smoke is a tar rose
blackening the walls,
there Picasso
bakes potter's clay
between the kiln's fiery racks
polishing it, breaking it
until clay becomes waist,
a siren's petal,
a moistened gold guitar.
And then with a paintbrush
he licks it,
and so comes the ocean

or the harvest.
Clay yields to him
her dark grape cluster
tightening her chalk hips.
Afterwards Picasso returns to his studio.
The little centaurs that await him
grow, they gallop.
Silence is born
in the iron goat's udders.
And Picasso enters his cave
leaving behind
scratched walls,
red stalactites
genital footprints.

And then in following hours
he speaks with the barber.

8

Ehremburg

So many rough-haired dogs,
small-snouted shiny-nosed,
tails behind some furniture,
and suddenly now more hair,
long grey locks, eyes
older than the world,
and one hand
upon the paper,
implanting peace,

overthrowing myths,
overturning fire and whistling,
or speaking of simple love
with the tenderness
of a poor baker.
It is Ehremburg.
It is his house in Moscow.
Oh how many times,
locked away in his house,
did I think it had no walls.
There between four walls
the river of life,
the human river
comes and goes leaving
lives, deeds, battles,
and ancient Ehremburg,
young Ilya,
with that river of earth and lives
he collects here and there
fragments, sparks,
waves, kisses, hats,
he crafts them all
like a wizard.
He throws it all into his oven,
by day and by night.
From there spring metals,
red swords,
great bread loaves of fire,
waves of anger, flags,
weapons for two centuries,
iron for millions,
and he very tranquil, rough-haired,
with his long grey locks,

smoking and full
of ash.

From time to time
he leaves the oven
and just when you think
he's going to explode,
you see him walking,
smiling,
with the most wrinkled pants in the world:
he is going to plant a jasmine
at his country house:
he digs the hole,
puts his hands in,
he handles the roots
as though they were made of silk,
he buries them,
he waters them,
and then with short steps,
with ash, with mud, with leaves,
with jasmine, with history,
with all things in the world
about mankind,
he moves away smoking.

If you want to know something
about jasmine trees,
write him a letter.

9

Words for Europe

I, an American from wretched lands,
metal mesas,
where the blow of man against man
joins that of Earth against man.
I, a wandering American,
orphan of the rivers and the
volcanoes that created me,
say to you, simple Europeans
of twisted streets,
humble owners of peace and olive oil,
wise men peaceful as smoke,
I say to you: I've come here
to learn from you,
from some and from others, from all,
because what good is
the world to me, why were
the sea and roads made,
except to go watching and learning
a little from all beings.
Don't shut the door
(like the black doors,
splattered with the blood
of my mother Spain).
Don't show me the enemy scythe
or the armor-plated squadron,
or the ancient gallows
for the new Athenian,
in the wide and worn streets

by the gleaming of the grapes.
I have no wish to see a dead young soldier
with his eyes eaten out.
Show me the infinite thread of life
passing through one country or another
weaving a spring suit.
Show me a pure machine,
steel blue beneath the thick olive,
ready to move through the wheat fields.
Show me the face filled with the roots
of Leonardo, because that face
is your geography,
and at the top of the mountains,
so many times described and painted,
your flags together
wave in
the electric wind.

Bring water from the fertile Volga
to the water of the golden Arno.
Bring white seeds
from the Polish resurrection,
and from your vineyards bring
sweet red fire to the snowy North!
I, an American, son
of the widest deserts of mankind,
came to learn life from you
and not death, not death!
I didn't cross the ocean,
or the deadly cordillera,
or the wild plague of Paraguay's prisons,
to see your eyeless sockets
your dried blood on the roads
together with myrtles I knew

from beloved books alone.
I've come instead to ancient honey
and new life's splendor.
I've come to your peace and your portals,
your burning lamps,
your weddings.
I've come to your solemn libraries
from so far away.
I arrive at your dazzling factories
to work a moment
and to eat among the workers.
I enter and leave your houses.
You will see me in Venice,
in beautiful Hungary,
in Copenhagen,
in Leningrad, speaking
with the young Pushkin, in Prague
with Fučik, with all the dead
and all the living, with all
green metals of the North
and carnations of Salerno.
I am the witness who arrives
to visit your home.
Offer me peace and wine.

I leave early tomorrow.

Spring awaits me everywhere.

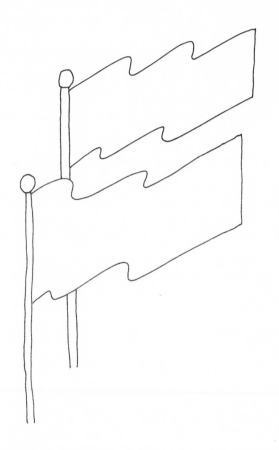

II

THE WIND IN ASIA

1

Flying to the sun

From the crinkled expanses
of the North, Northeast I went flying
as far as Peking oranged and green.
Below my flight Yan'an
was the lonely yellow shell
of a moon mineral and void.
The cars and the wind,
the aerial sun,
greeted the holy land,
the caves from which
liberty amassed its dust.
The heroes were no longer
wedged between the scars of the land:
their seed high and free

grew scattered and reunited.
The Gobi Desert's dry skin burned,
the regions of the lunar frontiers,
the sandy branches
of your wide world, China,
until the flight revealed
the prairies below,
the waters, the gardens,
and suddenly on your shore,
Peking ancient and new,
you welcomed me. Then
the sound of soil
and wheat
and spring,
footsteps on the roads,
streets infinitely peopled,
as if you had reunited
water's whole murmur
in a pure cup
lifting up to me
your people's lives:
keen whistles,
steel sounds,
rumble of sky and silk.
I lifted in my cup
your many lives
and the ancient silence.

It was the gift you gave me,
the strength of ancient stone singing,
of an old river nourishing
the young spring.

Suddenly I saw
the world's ancient tree
covered with flowers and fruit.
Suddenly I heard
life's river
pass by overflowing and steady
with crystal-clear language.
I drank clear strength
from your ancient goblet,
the new day:
a taste of star and earth was fixed
in my mouth. And I spied your face
among the faces,
young and ancient mother,
smiling,
there in your guerilla uniform
sowing seed
guarding safe the wheat
and your people's peace
with your armored smile
and your iron sweetness.

2

The parade

The people marched
before Mao Tse-tung.
None of them was
hungry and barefoot –
they who descended

the dry gorges,
they who live in caves,
they who eat roots,
and who, when they came down,
were steel wind,
steel wind of Yan'an and the North.
Today other men paraded,
smiling and sure,
resolute and joyful,
treading firmly the free earth
of the far wide fatherland.

And so passed
a proud young woman, dressed
in worker's blue,
and together with her smile,
like a snow waterfall,
forty thousand textile mouths,
the silk factories that march and smile,
the new car builders,
the old craftsmen of marble,
walking, walking,
before Mao,
all of vast China, seed by seed,
of iron grains,
and scarlet silk throbbing in the sky
like petals of the earthly rose
reunited at last,
and the great drum passed
before Mao,
and a dark thunder
went up from it
saluting him.
It was China's ancient voice,

the voice of leather,
the voice of buried time,
the old voice, the centuries
saluted him.
And then like a tree
of unexpected flowers
the children, by thousands,
saluted, and so
the new fruit and the old land,
time, wheat,
the flags of men reunited at last,
there they were.

There they were, and Mao smiled
because from the dry heights
of the North
this human river was born,
because from girls' heads
severed
by the North Americans
(or by Chiang, their lackey),
there in the plazas,
was this great life born.
Because from the Party's teaching,
in little books poorly printed,
came forth this lesson for the world.
He smiled, thinking on the harsh years
past,
the land filled with strangers, hunger
in the humble huts,
the Yang Tze showing on its back
steel reptiles

armor-plated
against the imperialist invaders,
the homeland sacked
and today, now,
the land cleansed,
vast China cleansed,
walking on its own soil.

Breathing the homeland
the men paraded
before Mao
and with new shoes
they pounded the earth,
parading,
while the wind in the red flags
played and on high
Mao Tse-tung stood smiling.

3

Giving a Medal to Madame Sun Yat Sen

The medal that Ehremburg
placed upon your chest
is a golden shoot harvested from the
great and peaceful Soviet land.

Your chest is worthy
of this blossom of gold,
Sung Sin Ling.

We have known you
since the days China awoke,
and then when once again
China was betrayed and martyred,
by her old enemies,
and from the first day we saw you
when China was freed,
there on the front line,
in the vanguard
with the liberators.
So we saw you, dear friend,
on arrival at the airport:
You seemed to us more youthful
than we had thought and more modest,
just like your people,
who have suffered and battled so
and who, in victory,
smile and salute all
the world's peoples.

We, Latin American men, we know
your enemies.
Our continent has riches – oil, copper,
sugar, nitrate, tin –
but it all belongs to our enemies,
the same ones
you've expelled forever.
Our peasants in fields and villages have
neither shoes nor culture, but
with their thefts these enemies have built
fifty-story homes in New York
and with our wealth fashioned weapons
to enslave other peoples.

Therefore the Chinese people's victory
is our victory.
Therefore all peoples love and respect new China.
Some diplomats in San Francisco and Washington
don't wish to "recognize"
the People's Republic of China.
They don't know it exists.
They might also not "recognize" the Earth –
and yet it moves,
moves forward, not back,
as they might wish.

The men in San Francisco
may not "recognize" new China,
but they might take a survey
throughout America
asking thousands of miners,
peasants, professors and poets,
the old and the young,
from Alaska to the South Pole, and
then they will get this answer:
"We recognize and love Mao Tse-tung.
He is our great brother."

Therefore, dear friend of peace,
Sung Sin Ling,
this golden shoot
from Stalin's bounteous land
now comes pinned to your chest,
woman guileless and great,
not by chance not caprice,
but from our love for you,
for the peace you defend,
not only for your people,

but that all people
might know one another
and build their lives in freedom.

4

Everything is so Simple

At dawn in the village
children and light welcome me.
The peasants showed me all
their conquered lands,
the communal harvest,
the granaries,
the ancient owner's homes.
They showed me the place
where poor mothers
threw their daughters over a cliff,
or sold them, not that long ago,
oh! not that long ago. Now it seems
a bad dream,
the plague, the hunger,
the North Americans,
the Japanese, the bankers
from London and France,
they all came to civilize
China tearing out her guts,
selling her on the World's Exchanges,
whoring her out in Shanghai.
They wished to make of her
a vast cabaret for the disembarking
troops, a place

of silk and hunger.
Skeletons piled themselves up
by the river,
villages wept
black smoke
and sickness.
"Aay! How is there room
in death
for so many Chinese dead,"
cried
the bourgeois dame
reading the newspapers.
By the river the dead were heaped
like ash mountains, hunger
strode China's roads
and in New York, Chiang Kai Shek
bought buildings,
a partner with Truman and Eisenhower.
The sad ancient fortress
smelled of opium and dung.
The prisons too,
filled with the dead.
Students beheaded
in a town plaza
on North American decree,
and all the while
Mme. Chiang Kai Shek
Life Magazine's darling
her photo lovelier each time.

Depart, damned dream!
Depart from China!
Depart from the world!

Come to the village with me!

I enter
and see the granaries,
the smile
of China liberated:
the peasants
distributing the land.
From Yan'an
freedom flowed down
with the bare feet and broken shoes
of peasant and soldier.
O China's freedom,
you are my muse,
dressed in blue
on a dusty road.
Unable to wash yourself
or dry your blood
yet you march and march
the dark land marching with you:
forgotten Bolivia marches
for freedom, Chile marches,
Iran as well,
they all will enter the village with you,
with my muse.
Little girls dressed
in guerilla blue,
muse of the wind,
of the free lands,
to you I sing: to the leather ammo belt
and your rifle,
to your dry mouth,
I sing.

Sing, muse,
enter all the world's streets
with fire and dust,
sweat and blood.
There will yet be time
to wash yourself, but advance now,
forward, advance!

I saw everything
in free China's village.
Nothing had to be said.
Children poured around me,
making sure I didn't just pass by.
I ate their rice, their fruit,
I drank their pale rice wine.
Everything they showed me
they showed
with the same pride
I saw in Romania,
in Poland,
in Hungary,
a peasant's resurgent pride
at the dawning
of tomorrow's world
who first sees flour,
fruit,
wheat growing,
and then
though he be older than the world itself
shows you rice and grapes,
hen's eggs,
knows not what to say.
All is now theirs
for the first time.

All rice,
all land,
all of life.

How easy it is
when one has obtained
happiness, how simple
everything is.
When you and I, my love, kiss,
how easy to be happy.

But you forget
how long you wandered
without finding me
how many times
you lost your way
until you fell down, tired.
And, well,
you didn't know
that I also wandered seeking you,
that my heart nearly lost its way
to bitterness
emptiness.
We didn't know then
that had we marched
forward, forward,
straight on, straight on,
always, always,
we would find each other.
And that's what happens to nations:
they don't always know,
they don't always understand,

they make mistakes,
but always move forward
to find,
find themselves,
just as you found me,
and then it all seems easy,
but it was not so easy
to walk blind.

They had to learn about life,
about the enemy,
about darkness,
and in his writings,
there was Mao teaching
there was the Party
severe and tender,
and now we young Chinese men
from the fields,
young muse,
do not forget:
all seems as easy as water.
That's not true.
The struggle is not water,
it is blood.
It comes from afar.
There are the dead:
our fallen brothers.
The whole road
is filled with the dead
and we will not forget.
And the village
is not calm,
the air is not calm,
it brings words,

songs,
faces,
days past,
prisons,
walls splashed with blood
and now the village is sweet,
victory is sweet.

Let us raise a glass
to the muse,
to those whom we do not forget
and to those who rebuild,
to those who fell
and continue living
everywhere,
because the world is wide
and in all places always
blood flowed,
the same:
our blood.
Now
I enter the village
of the free country
and the air is sweet
as never before
and I breathe life,
the land,
victory.

The land is the same,
if we stretch
our hands over its skin,
here or in Patagonia

or the isles of the sea.
The land is always
the same,
and now
entering your village,
the smell of bread,
the smell of smoke,
the smell of wheat,
the smell of water and wine,
it is my land,
it is the whole land.
And then with respect
I saluted
the ancient land,
its beauty,
its vast farmland,
its face of dust and dew,
the brilliant freedom
in its smile,
and I thought
upon my far shores,
my flag,
my sand, my surf,
upon all my stars.
And so that morning
in the Chinese village
I entered singing,
because my heart
was as a guitar
all strings sounding
remembering my country,
they sang
remembering my homeland,
there, in America.

When once I arrive
at the people's home
in a free land,
everything
will seem so simple,
so easy,
like the kiss we now
give each other,
my love.

5

The cicadas

Cicadas crying out
shrill in the autumn
filled the village morning.
I approached: and cicadas held captive
in their little cages,
children's companions, sounded
China's boundless cello
throughout the small village,
its murmuring
golden motion.

Scarcely had I spied the prisoners
among their tiny
fresh bamboo cells,
when I returned to leave –

but the peasants placed
the insect castle
in my hands instead.

I remember from my childhood
the workers
on the train where my father labored,
the raging children
exposed to the elements, barely
clothed in rags,
their faces battered by rain or sand,
foreheads crossed
by harsh scars,
and they brought me
blue partridge eggs,
green beetles,
moon-colored Spanish flies,
and all that treasure
from great battered hands
to my child hands,
all that
made me laugh and cry,
think and sing,
there in the rainy
forests
of my childhood.

And now
these cicadas
in their castle of fragrant bamboo
from the depth of China's land,
scraping their strident
gold note,
arrived in my hands

from hands baptized
by freedom-conquering
gunpowder
from the wide free lands,
the hands of the people,
great hands,
into my hands leaving
their treasure.
And so I remembered my childhood
as through the land
I went pondering
singing,
but nothing,
nothing like this,
this living treasure.
And then they walked with me,
my companions
all my days in China.

In the morning, in my hotel room,
thirty cicadas
spoke my name
with a sharp sound
of green steel
and I gave them leaves
and they ate,
poking from their little cages painted
guerrilla masks, and in the afternoon,
when over the vast lands
the sun set,
and yet once more the day affirmed
the people's freedom in their homeland.

In my window
the cicadas with a single metallic
voice
sang
toward the fields,
toward the children,
toward the other cicadas,
toward the leaves and toward the huts,
toward the whole land:
chanting goodbye to the day
in the incredible height of their song,
and so, from my window,
by day and by night,
they saluted you, China,
one voice from the land
that the people's hands
entrusted to me,
a multiplied voice singing
with me, along your roads.

6

China

China, your painted image in the West
forever a wizened crone,
infinitely poor,
clutching an empty rice bowl,
crouching at a temple door.

From every nation
soldiers came and went on the walls,

sacking you like an ownerless house,
and to the world you were exotic scents,
a mixture of tea and ashes,
while at the door of the temple
with your empty
plate, you gazed on us
with an ancient gaze.
In Buenos Aires they painted
and sold your portrait
to cultured women,
while in lecture halls
your magic syllables
surged upwards quickly
as from buried light.

Everyone knew something
about your dynasties
and upon saying "Ming" or "Celadon"
pursed their lips
as if they had eaten a strawberry,
and so they wished you to be for us
a land without men, a homeland
where the wind whooshed
through empty temples
and left singing, alone,
through the mountains.

They wished us to believe
you would sleep,
sleep an eternal sleep,
you the "inscrutable one,"
untranslatable, strange,
a mendicant mother with silken rags,

while from each one of your ports
departed ships laden with treasures
and the buccaneers fought
among themselves over
your heritage: minerals
and marble, planning,
after bleeding you dry,
how they would carry off
a fine ship laden with your bones.

7

The Great March

But something was happening in the world.
Your portrait did not satisfy us.
Your majestic poverty was lovely,
but it wasn't enough for us.
The Soviet flag rippled
kissed by gunpowder
between the hearts of men.
You, China, we missed you,
and across the seas
we quickly heard
that the voice of the wind
no longer sang alone
along your broad roads.

Mao arose
and through the length
and breadth of China
we saw his shoulders rise

out of such suffering,
enveloped by the dawn.
From far away, from America,
by whose shore
my people hear each wave of the sea,
we saw his calm head arise,
and his shoes turn themselves
to the North.
Toward Yan'an in dusty suit
he turned his vast movement:
and we saw from then
that the stripped lands
of China yielded men to him,
small men, wrinkled old men,
childlike smiles.

We saw life.

The ancient land was not alone.
It was not the water moon
filling the spectral ancient land.
From each stone a man,
a new heart with a rifle,
and we saw you China,
peopled by your soldiers,
your own at last, eating grass,
without bread, without water,
marching the long day
that dawn might be born.

8

The Giant

You were neither mystery
nor heavenly jade.
You were like us, plain people,
and when bare feet and shoes,
peasant and soldier, marched
in the distance
defending your integrity,
we saw the face,
we saw the hands
of one who worked iron, our hands,
and on the long road we perceived
your people's names: they were ours.
They sounded otherwise, but beneath
the sharp syllables,
they were in the end the faces and the steps
that marched with Mao
through the desert and the snow
to save the seed
of our own spring.

Tall was the giant
measuring step by step
his rice, his bread, his land, his dwelling,
recognized by the peoples of the world:
"How quickly you've grown, brother!"
But his enemy watched him as well.
From the grey banks
of New York and the City

the money pockets there
that feed on blood
said to themselves
with fear: "Who is this?"

The calm giant didn't answer:
He saw
the broad hard lands of China.
He gathered
with one hand all the grief
and misery,
and with the other
showed forth
morning's red wheat,
all that the land would yield,
and on his great face grew
a smile that rippled in the wind,
a smile like grain,
a smile like golden stars
above all the spilled blood.
And so your banners were lifted.
Now the people saw you cleanse
your vast land,
unity, threatening hurricane,
hammer over evil,
light conquering
the old enemy, victorious.

9

Sheaves for You

O Republic,
you extended broad arms
across your body
and established peace as your destiny!
And those who ventured from beyond the sea,
wicked, to rape and ransack –
you received them well – now bound
in fetters to Formosa they fly
to feed the scorpions' nest.
But upon Korea they fell. Blood
and sorrow and destruction,
their normal fare:
empty walls, dead women,
but soon
the fortress of your volunteers
arrived one day
to rescue mankind's sacred brotherhood.
Sea to sea, land to snow,
all men gaze on you, China.
What a powerful young sister
has been born to us!

The American man, bent in his furrow,
surrounded by the metal
of his burning machine,
the poor man of the tropics,
the valiant Bolivian miner,
the broad worker of deep Brazil,

the shepherd of unbounded Patagonia,
they gaze upon you, People's China,
they salute you and with me
they send you this kiss upon your brow.

You are not the image they wished for us:
that of a blind beggar by the temple,
but instead a strong and sweet
captain of the people,
even with your victorious weapons
in one hand
harvest sheaves held across your breast
and over your head
the star of all peoples!

III

THE SIREN RETURNED

1

I sing and declare

From the Baltic summer,
blue steel, amber and foam,
to where the Carpathians
crown the temples of Poland,
Europe's pale diadems,
I crossed the land
of martyrdoms and births,
skin drawn and quartered,
the infinite reborn wheat,
the coal caverns, and they showed me
ancient blood on the snow,
the prairies scraped clean,
a man and his kitchen, buried,
a babe in his tiny pram,

a flower over his mother's bones.
I witness to those days
I feel and I sing
but at this time
I have no golden strings.
The harp and its sweetness burned
with the world's fire.
But now I come to proclaim
and sing rebirth from the dead.
Receive me,
see what I lift from the silken land,
a bit of violin, a dead ring
and that which is forgotten.
Accept what I bring,
song and story,
because I bring in my sack
not only buried blood,
ruins, weeping and ash
but the grey rain of the North:
above newly-sown fields
it falls and falls,
and so grows bread without ending
as never was before.
The hammer pounds,
the shovel rises and falls,
stones sound in the new buildings,
life rises.

Oh Poland,
Oh love,
Oh spring,
come with me
and let me open for you
tales and ballads

along all the roads,
and in the depth,
beyond the dead,
life sings and tells tales,
and all this, the song and story
you taught me,
Poland, that is what I now teach:
faith in life, deeper
when it has come from far away,
from death, faith in mankind
when it is able to
triumph over itself,
faith in a home
born from wide ashes,
faith in a song that could be sung
when there is no longer
mouth or voice!
Poland, you taught me to live
anew
to sing anew
with my guitar
out from its case
this pilgrim ode:
the indestructible flower
and the new hope,
ancient sorrows buried,
the rebuilding of joy.

2

Spring in the North

I travelled through
Poland's green and steamy spring.
Wheat grains trembled in the abundant
light, milk flowed
as a white river
to the sea
from collective farms,
humid fields, the scent of soil,
flowers rose like blue lamps
quick pinpoints of blood.
And from the long winter the pines
moved their ship's flanks
as though embarking on the spring,
while below, stirring in the shade,
strawberries half-opened their buds.

I found the air metallic,
fresh with the air of rebirth,
because it wasn't just forest,
sea and land,
but mankind arising
there from the dead.
This time the Flood flowed blood
and the struggle's hidden ark
wound its way along the dead.
Therefore Poland's violent
spring was
iron in my mouth,

electric liquid,
the kiss of the land,
the heart of mankind
in the starry cup of life!

3

Ruins on the Baltic

Gdansk, pockmarked by war,
roses shredded,
a ghost among ghosts,
between the ocean's scent
and the high white sky,
I walked among your ruins,
between bits of tarnished silver.
The fog came in with me,
glacial mists,
and wandering
I disentangled streets
without homes and without people.
I know war
and that eyeless lipless face,
those dead windows
I know,
I saw them in Madrid, in Berlin,
in Warsaw,
but that Gothic nave
with its red brick ash
by the sea, in the port

of ancient voyages,
that merchant ship figurehead,
green ship of the cold waters,
with its heart-piercing crevasses,
its walls mere stumps,
its pride demolished,
entered my soul
like a gust of snow, dust and smoke,
something blinding, desperate.
The guildhall
with its fallen emblems,
the banks in which gold tinkled
falling down the throat of Europe
the red piers
where a river
of grain landed
like an earthly wave
summer's scent,
all was dust, mountains
of shattered substance,
and the iron Baltic wind
flew through the void.

4

Peace building

But there was also
life.
In other places and at other times
in my life death

waited for me on the corners.
Here life awaits.
I have seen life in Gdansk
replenishing itself.
Cars kissed me
with steel lips
Water quivered.
I have seen cranes pass stately
like castles over the water,
cranes of maritime iron,
newly built.
I have seen a giant
scrap mass crushed
iron upon iron
beaten
give birth little by little
to the cranes' form,
and awake from the depths of death
the majestic blue of the shipyard.
I have seen with my eyes
the wave's dew
multiply in the ships' rebirth,
the prows tacking
helmed by a man newly disinterred.
I have seen
how a port is born,
not from seas and lands
washed and lustrous,
but from disaster.
I have seen you born, titanic dove,
white and blue, the fleet,
and watched you lift yourself
flying firm and strong

away from the tangled destruction
and the bloody solitude
of wind and ashes!

5

The forests

Toward the cold forests and lakes
of the green North,
Masurian lakes,
spreading to all parts,
wide ponds suffused
by pale sky,
lagoons like needles,
placid water forms all
remained there as if a star
had broken to pieces
or a green moon
had fallen in drops from on high.
The air is comely, and the wind
combs the bristled locks
of steely pines.
Comely is the air, fresh
and blue beneath the pines.

Suddenly you saw the wind
its trembling cloak
of oxygen and needles.
The wind is solemn in the jungle.
It makes small sounds

like fallen missives,
or the bottle's cry as wind
crosses its lips
or pebbles breaking,
fragments of wood
scraped with a father's hands,
it blows and rises
from one tree to another
startling the birds.

The North wind is fair,
brother to the snow,
deep within the pines.
And I walk without a hat.
The air
crowns my head with cold,
fresh lips bite me.
I enter the green freshness
singing
as on the high sea.
I sing
and tread the grass
newly endowed
with small yellow stars.
Fair North of broad shoulders,
lakes and pines,
I salute you:
let me breathe you,
walk between the pines and the waters
singing and whistling
and rest on your wet carpet
like a fallen tree
beneath your green dream.

6

The siren returned

My love, if one day
you died,
and I dug
and dug
within your tomb
night and day
to compose you anew,
lift your breasts from the dust,
the mouth I adored from its ashes,
build again
your arms your legs your eyes,
your locks of twisted metal,
and breath life into you
with the love that loves you,
grant you to walk again,
pulse again hip to hip –
even so, my love, they gave new life
to Warsaw.

And I would come as one blind
to your ashes but seeking you,
lifting little by little
your body's sweet form –
so they too found
but wind and ash
in their beloved city
razed fragments,
coals crying in the rain,

a woman's smile
beneath the snow.
Beauty had died,
windows shattered,
night lay down above the white dead,
day lighted an empty meadow.

And so they raised her up,
with love, and so they came
blind and sobbing,
but they dug deep,
cleansed the ash.
It was late, night time,
weariness, snow
stayed the shovel,
but digging they found
first the head,
the white breasts
of the sweet dead one,
her siren's clothing,
at last her heart beneath the ground,
buried and burned but alive,
and today alive she lives,
throbbing in the
midst of her beauty's rebirth.

Now you see how
love built avenues,
made the moon sing in the gardens.
Today when
flake to flake falls the snow
upon the roofs and the bridges
and winter beats

the doors of Warsaw,
the fire, the song – all these live again
in the homes that love built over death.

Ay for those who fled and thought
to escape with poetry:
they don't know that love is in Warsaw,
and death
was there defeated,
and when the river passes,
it quickens people, destiny –
like twin flowers of perfume and silver,
city and poetry,
Warsaw and poetry,
in her bright domes
they guard the light, the fire,
the bread of their fate.

Miraculous Warsaw,
buried heart
newly alive and free,
city of proof
that mankind is greater
than all misery,
Warsaw, let me
touch your walls –
they aren't build with stone or wood
but hope,
and he who wishes to touch hope,
strong and hard,
stubborn land that sings,
metal that rebuilds,
indestructible sand,

boundless grain,
honey for all the ages,
eternal hammer,
conquering star,
invincible tools,
life's matrix,
hope,
let him touch and
feel how
through hope rise again
your life and blood,
because love, Warsaw,
lifted your siren form
and if I touch your walls,
your holy skin,
I understand
that you are life
and within your walls
death, at last, has died.

7

Polish song

There war in the
great forests' depths,
war by the water
slow yet growing
leapt out to assault me, in the midst
of peace
in the sylvan kingdom:
there it was.

Goering had left behind
his cement buckets,
the horrid architecture
inhuman, jagged,
half-open slits
like a reptile's eyes, naked forms
of cruelty, there, hidden,
in the wild beasts' new hovels
they planned to attack
Soviet light.
There from the shadow
they attacked the star
united all repulsive force,
the maggots and the venom,
destructive flames,
death's plans.
Already the forest in dark splendor
began to cover
these evil relics,
but there the crouching forts,
the broken nets that hid them
there still remained
the voice of dreadful metal,
the toothless mouth of war.

As today in the calm clear salons
of North American
military schools,
with steadfast precision
germ power
is studied
ready to spew its load of vomit
on villages
ready to murder children with water –

so schemes of fire
and murder were hatched
in cold forest grottos.

But the murderous wave halted
against a stone wall:
the uniform rampart
of socialism, the weight
of Stalin's fist,
and from the snowy East
peace returned to the forest.
The invaders who departed hence
did not return, but
the luminous air
of Stalingrad came,
it crossed Poland's forests,
opened the doors
of the bleeding invader
and from then on grew
forest vines,
and water awaits the fallen leaves,
electric squirrels
dance with new coats.
Dense liquid air
fills the land's cup,
my steps sink in the moss
as if I walked on oblivion,
a fragment of kindling
filled with things that stick to you
as a violin full of music,
leaves weave threads that cross
from one tree to another
threading the punctured

silence of the forest.

At the forest's foot the plains
sense wheat's birth,
farther on coal runs
to steel,
cities populate,
mankind marches,
men march,
navies grow,
at night the sky displays
its great starry light
to Poland saying: "Men of all
lands and seas,
look how
our steel daughter grows."

And the moon is astonished
because today from yesterday's
charred empty shell
a roof reflects
sweet nocturnal light,
sun enters the bakeries
early,
sits down in the schools,
lives life, builds mankind,
the tough arm circles
the dove's waist.

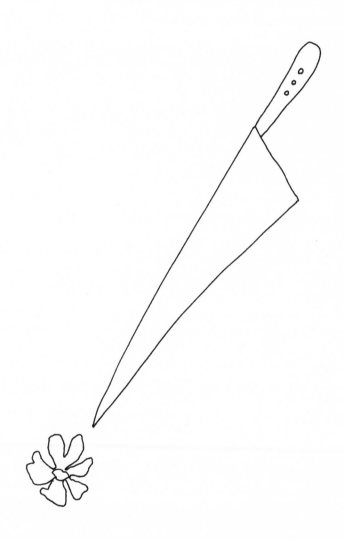

IV

THE LOST GOATHERD

Return, Spain

Spain violet heart Spain,
you've abandoned my breast,
gone not as the waistless sun
but like salt in the throat,
bread in the teeth, hatred
in the black beehive, the day
above dawn's somersaults,
not even that, but like the weave
of a visceral element, a deep
eyelid that sees not and yields not,
mineral land, a rose made of bone
castle-like, open in my mind.
How can I call except with your mouth?

What other lips can be my advocate?

Are you bereft or is it I who am mute?

What does your silenced field say?

Where shall I go without your voice, sand mother?

What am I without your crucified beacon?

Where am I without water from your rock?

Who are you if you did not give me blood?

O torment! Restore me, receive me
before my fame and tender shoots
disappear in the spring.
I am drawn to you – my destiny lies chained
to your outraged solitudes, to the weight
of your victory.

Spain, you are haughtier than a festal day,
than a prophecy, than torture,
and the cruel tower
of your lost voice matters not, but only hard
resistance, the stone that sustains.

But why, if I am your sand,
the water in your waters, the blood in your wounds,
do you deny me now the voice that calls me,
your voice, the ground of all my being?

I call upon all that is in you,
my own life's heart,

though torn by knives,
open yourself today, rising beyond misfortune,
light of your countenance
rise up, piercing the sky,
breaking the night gloom and the zodiac stars,
and surge, flour and dawn,
a flaming moon above the bone yards.

You will kill. Kill, Spain, sainted virgin,
arise, grasping tenderness
like a blind rose set free
above the hellish jewels.

Come to me, give me back the tower
they stole,
give me back the language
and the people who await me, astound me
with the harmony of your lasting beauty.
Lift yourself up in your blood and your fire:
the blood that you gave, the first,
and the fire, nest of your holy light.

1

If I should recall you

Spain, you have no keepsakes for me,
you have no memory.
If I wish to recall
the orange blossoms,

or the yellow market
or Valencia's acid shadows,
I furl my forehead,
I open my eyes
and I bite my mouth.
No, I have no keepsakes.
I want nothing of your dry form
or your sweeping hair,
I don't want your fresh spring leaves
nor wish to gather them
along the melancholy road.
I want you pure, complete,
restored to me
with deeds and words,
with all your senses,
unlaced and free,
metallic and open!
Granada red and firm,
black topaz, Spain,
my love, hipbone
and skeleton of the world,
incandescent guitar,
fire that doesn't destroy, oh doleful
and beloved stone,
my heart would bleed out
seeking to recall you to mind –
and I need blood to recapture
your loveliness,
that your silence may
kneel
conquered, ended,
and your people's voice
be heard again
in the world's new chorus.

2

Our brother will arrive

Something is happening,
fermenting, tears,
moons, pains, sorrows.
A warning that
something's happening,
a dot, something
like a scarlet-colored comet:
all your stars,
Spain,
your men, your women,
Spain.
There is an ocean,
a vast electric wind
forming lightning bolts,
something growing in your womb,
Spain.
We recognize
the brother who comes,
lift him up to the light,
nourish him with your blood,
so that he can run
though scarcely born,
that he can die
now,
give him
milk from a wild stone,
atomic earth power,
give all your bones,

the bones that don't forget,
give him the open sockets
of our bullet-riddled men,
give him your life and mine,
if you wish,
and then,
give him knives,
hidden rifles.
The spider
beneath your bed,
look
in the cemeteries,
seize weapons from the air,
and let him fight,
Spain, let your son fight,
let your son fight, Spain.

Break
your prison, open
your eyes,
lift up
your ancient heart
because there is your banner,
the new star in the midst
of your shed blood.
Rise up
and cry out,
rise up
and cast down,
rise up and build,
harvester,
fling your son to the world,
knead your bread once more,
the land awaits

your hands and your flour.
It is your victory we lack,
that we seek before sleeping,
that we yearn for
before waking.
Your forgotten victory
goes wandering in the streets,
let it enter,
let your victory enter,
open the doors,
let your son open the door
with stout red miner's hands,
that the doors of Spain may open,
because this is the victory
we lack
and without that victory
there is no honor in the land.

3

The lost goatherd

His name was Miguel.
He was a young
goatherd by the outskirts
of Orihuela. I loved him
and placed my hand on his chest,
he grew in stature
until his song stood out in the rough
Spanish land

like a sharp oak
with all the buried nightingales conjoined,
all the birds in sonorous Heaven,
the splendor of a man twinned
in love with his beloved,
the scented buzz
of the golden bee hives,
the bitter birth smell
of newborn goats,
the scent of pure red cigars.
Miguel made of all this –
soil and bee,
bride, wind and soldier –
clay for his conquered race,
people's poet,
and so he went, treading
upon the thorns of Spain
with a voice that
her hangmen
now must hear, they listen,
they whose hands are
spotted with his indelible blood,
they hear his song
and they think
it's just soil
and water.
That's not true.
It's blood,
blood,
Spanish blood,
blood of all Spain's people,
and your blood sings out
names names
cries out

names all things
because he loved all,
but that voice doesn't forget,
that blood doesn't forget, it
knows whence it comes
and for whom it sings.
It sings
that prisons be opened
that liberty walks the streets.
It calls to me
to show me all the places
they dragged him,
even him,
the people's light,
tongues' lightning flash,
it shows me
Ocaña's presidio,
where drop by drop
they bled him,
where they cut
his throat,
where for seven years
they killed him
soaking themselves in blood
with his own song
because when they silenced
those lips
so died the lamps of Spain.
And so he cries out and says to me:
"Here, this is where
they slowly put me to death."
So he who loved and carried
beneath his miserable clothes

all Spain's springs
was murdered beneath
the shade of the walls
while the bells tolled
in the hangman's honor,
but
in those days
the orange blossoms
gave forth their scent
to the world
and that aroma was
the martyred heart
of the goatherd of Orihuela
and Miguel was his name.

While he suffered in those
days and years
history's light
was buried,
but its heart still beats
and tomorrow returns.
Those days and centuries
when jailers meted out
torture and agony
to Miguel Hernández,
the land was bereft of
his goatherd's steps upon the mountains
and the dead guerrillero,
on falling, victorious,
let a murmur loose from the land
to rise up, a heartbeat,
as if the stars half-opened themselves
from a silent jasmine:
it was Miguel's poetry.

He spoke from the soil,
from the soil
he will speak forever,
it is his people's voice,
he went among the soldiers
like a burning tower.

He was a fortress
of songs and thunder,
he was like a baker:
with his hands he crafted
his sonnets.
All his poetry
is like porous soil,
drinking the rain –
grains, sand,
mud and wind –
and it has the form
of a Levantine vase,
filled to the brim,
of a queen bee's belly,
it has the scent
of clover in the rain,
of amaranth ash,
of dung smoke, late,
upon the hills.
His poetry is corn gathered
in golden cluster,
a vineyard of black grapes,
a bottle of dazzling crystal
filled with wine and water,
night and day,
it is a scarlet branch,

the Morning Star,
hammer and sickle
written with diamonds
in the shadow of Spain.

Miguel Hernández,
your land and people
will live again with you,
their orange-colored clay,
their yeast.
You guarded Spain
with your rough hand,
in agony,
because you were made
for dawn and victory,
of water and her virgin soil,
of insatiable amazement,
of plants and nests.
You were
song's unconquerable sprouting,
the homeland of integrity
resolute against the enemies,
both Moor and Francoista,
one heavy hand filled
with vines and metal.
With invisible sword in arms,
you died,
but not alone.
It wasn't only the burnt grass
on the poor hills of Orihuela
that spread through the world
your voice and your scent.
Your people seemed
mute,

not seeing
not hearing your death
or the scornful Masses
but now go,
go ask
and see if anyone
doesn't know your name.

Everybody knew,
in the jails,
while the jailers
dined with Cossio,
your name.
It was a wet brightness
through the tears
your wild honey voice.
Your revolutionary
poetry
was, in silence, in cells,
of one prison or another,
repeated,
treasured,
and now
the seed sprouts,
your grain comes to light,
your violent grain
accuses,
in each street,
your voice takes the road
of the rebellions.
No one, Miguel, has forgotten you.
Here we all bear you
in the midst of our breast.

My son, you remember
when
I took you and placed
my stone-solid friendship
in your hands?
And well, now,
dead,
you give it all back to me.
You have grown and grown,
you are,
you are eternal,
you are Spain,
you are your people,
and they cannot kill you.
You have already lifted up
your granary breast,
your head
filled with red rays,
they have not stopped you now.
Now
like monks
they wish to bend the knee
belated in your remembrance,
they wish to sprinkle your face
with spit, Communist guerrillero.
They cannot.
We will not let them.
Now
stay pure,
stay silent,
keep your voice,
let them
pray,

let
the thin black stream trickle
from their putrid biers
and medieval mouths.
They know nothing else.
Your wind
will yet arrive,
the people's wind,
the face of Dolores,
the victorious advance
of our undying
Spain,
and then,
archangel of the goats,
fallen shepherd,
great poet of your people,
my son,
you will see your worn face
in the banners,
your visage victorious,
revived when the people revive,
marching with us
with none able
to separate you from the lap of Spain.

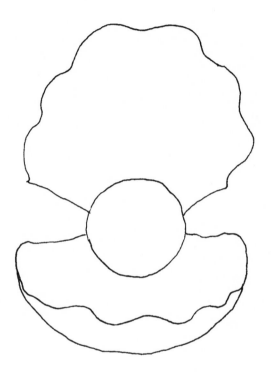

V

PRAGUE CONVERSATION

For Julius Fučík

1

My friend along the road

On Prague's streets each winter's day
I passed the walls of the stone house
where they tortured Julius Fučík.
The house says nothing,
stone the color of winter,
iron bars, deaf windows.
But each day I passed by,
looked, touched the wall,
sought an echo,
a word, the voice, the pure footprint
of the hero.
And so I saw his face come out one time,

and his hands another afternoon,
and then his whole being
accompanying me,
crossing through Wenceslas Plaza,
my good friend with me
by the old Havelska Market,
by the Starhov Garden,
from where Prague rises like a grey rose.

2

So it should have happened

And so it should have happened,
so it would have happened,
if you had not, nearly invisible,
entered forever into history.
We would have seen
each other every day,
we would have exchanged
certain books we love,
I would have told you tales
of fishermen and miners
from my seafaring homeland,
and we would have laughed
in such a way that passersby
would have found
our great joy dangerous.

3

You did it

There have been many men,
many Fučíks
who lived life well.
You, Julius Fučík,
did so.
The small and great painful duties
and the needful
small deeds,
to perform, to fulfill:
uprightness is a focused dot
that is repeated
until it becomes a line,
a norm, a path,
and you made that point
like all pure men
out of duty and joy,
because so we must be.

4

The duty of dying

But when the clock at long last
tolled death you complied,
complied with the same joyful peace,

complied with the duty of dying.
Nothing stood between your life and your death:
you built a single unbroken line,
a line still living,
straight and growing
advancing, advancing always,
from your death to other lives,
advancing, advancing always,
accumulating people, lives,
as a great river
fills itself from other rivers,
as sound
enriches and lifts music,
so your voice, your life continue
advancing through the whole world.
They are not inherited but living blood,
not memory but firm action,
you the human hero,
not a stone demigod,
one who filled his frame
with life's full content and
not his life alone
but all our lives,
and your freedom was not just two wings
on a coat of arms,
nor a dead statute,
but the firm hand of the Party
that sustains yours
and so from your strength,
growing in you from many others,
new lives regathered
and sowed seeds.
Men advanced
from the minute your countenance fell

in battle, and we dyed our flag
with the sacred blood
of your invincible heart.

5

You were life

Through the streets of Prague
your figure,
not that of a winged god,
but the pale persecuted face
that smiles on us after death.
The hero wearing
on his motionless head
not the laurels of forgotten stone,
but an old hat
and in his pocket the final
message of the Party,
the underground at midnight
the unionized dawn,
the pamphlet stained
with fresh ink,
and so street to street
Fučík, with your orders,
Fučík, with your pamphlets,
with your old hat,
with neither pride
nor humility, steeling
the armies of the resistance,

and walking toward death
with the peacefulness of a passerby
who ought to see it on the next corner,
through the streets of Prague's
ancient pearl winter,
while the enemy in the castle
howls at his pack of hounds,
from one street to another street
you organized
your people, unity, the victory
that today crowns your homeland's peace.

6

You are everywhere

Fučík's heritage, lineage
of silent joys,
you spread throughout the Earth
the iron indestructible man.
Korea, beloved land, you proved to
Philadelphia's bestial invaders
that Fučík's heritage, above the ash,
above the fire and the martyrdom,
continues aflame and conquers death.
Far away, in Paraguay dark
and poisonously green,
jailed children,
persecuted in the jungle,
falling on the bloodied
leaves, by the river,

closed forever Fučík's same
superhuman mouth.

In Iran the oil
returns to the people's hands
writing with red letters
your name, Julius of Prague.
And the Vietnamese girl
who with sweet flower hands
cradles her machine gun
carries in her purse torn
by the jungle's thorns
your book in characters
you could not read:
the book that in the last days
Athens' condemned
carried written on their noble faces
so the assassins
might find
your words anew
on dusted blood.

7

If I speak to them....

Thousands of years ago a man was crucified,
he died in his faith, thinking beyond Earth.
His cross weighed upon human life
and kneaded together anguish and hope.

We have millions of crucified ones
and our hope is here on Earth.
Let whomever wishes to see lift up his eyes.
Give me your hand if you wish to touch it.
Our hope is in China's new rice fields.
And when the white teeth of rice smile,
isn't the land joyous?
Aren't wheat and meat, a school,
a clean house, labor certain and just,
peace for children, love,
the book joining joy and wisdom,
aren't these mankind's conquests,
and these simple truths our hope?
Why should I go tomorrow
to the Aymara Indians, to the wretched of Bolivia,
frayed by the hunger and cold of its great heights
and promise them Heaven?
You wouldn't crucify me if they stayed hungry,
but if I were to speak to them of the cooperative
farm
I saw in Poland,
where milk, bread and book were common
treasures,
then you would lance a pole between my ribs
and crucify me, if my own did not defend me.
We find them crucified mile after mile, even
in prosperous New York, near the Stork Club,
they crucify men both black white every day.
But we will not calmly await
martyrdom or incense,
we will fight each day of our lives,
we will conquer and now we summon you,
just as from his gallows or his cross –
the name doesn't matter to me –
the dead heart of Julius Fučík defeats his killers.

8

Radiant Julius

Radiant Julius - from the honeycomb of lives
cell iron and sweet, made of honey and fire! –
give us this day as our daily bread
your essence, your presence,
your simple honesty and pure radiance.
Come to us today, tomorrow, forever,
because, simple hero,
you are the architecture
of tomorrow's man.
When death struck you down, the light
shone over the planet
with your eyes' bee color,
the germ of honey and battle,
sweetness and hardship,
all remained implanted
in mankind's life.
Your decision destroyed fear,
and your tenderness, the darkness.
You entered, naked man,
into the mouth of our inferno
and with beaten body,
intact, your stature was unbroken
and you kept the living truth
in the face of death.

9

With my friend from Prague

Your joyful land, Czechoslovakia,
steel-eyed mother, favored petal
of Europe, crowned
by your people's peace!
Sweet hills, waters, red roofs,
trembling like green rain,
the hop lifts its vertical threads,
while in Gotwaldov a hive
of intelligence and reason sustains
the new rose of human labor.
Oh, Fučík, come,
visit with me
your homeland's clean soil,
green, white and gold,
and in it enlightening it,
the clarity of the people!
Honor to the new furrow
to the new working day,
to Kladno's invincible steel!
To the new man who enters
the workshops and in the plazas,
to the sturdy new bridges
spanning the old river's turmoil,
thanks to Fučík, my friend,
my silent companion,
who was with me showing me all
in the winter color of Prague,
with his old invisible hat

and his sweet mute smile,
through life and death,
the heritage and the gift he gave us.
Julius Fučík, I salute you,
Czechoslovakia renewed,
mother of upright youth,
land of the silenced heroes,
republic of cloud and crystal,
grape bunch, bursting shoots, steel, people!

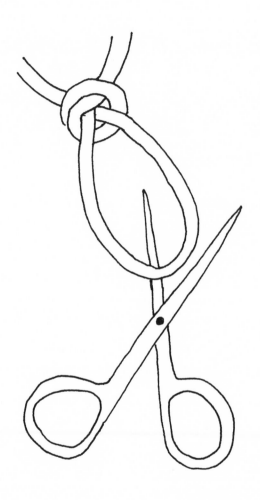

VI

THE WIDE NEW WORLD

With you through the streets

I wish to tell and sing
of the broad Russian land.
Only a few small things,
for I cannot fit it all into my song.
Humble deeds, plants,
people,
birds,
the works of men.
Many have always existed,
others
are being born,
because this is the land
of infinite birth.
And so I begin, walking
with you through the streets,

through the fields,
near the sea in winter.
You are my friend, come, let us walk together.

1

History changes

It was in Pushkin's time,
the flat spring land,
a wave of air
like the pure sail
of a ship transparent
glided through the meadow
lifting grass
and the seedlings' scent.
Near Leningrad fir trees
dance a slow waltz,
the sea's horizon.
Toward the East marched
trucks, energy,
boys and girls.
The steppe shook,
lambs piercing snow
in the immense and tender expanse.

The vast Soviet Union,
like no other land,

with room
for both the smallest blue flower
and the factory immense.
Great rivers tremble and sing
over its wide skin,
there lives
the sturgeon wrapped in silver
guarding roe clusters
of freshness and delight.
The bear in the mountains
with delicate feet
moves like an ancient monk at daylight
in a green basilica.
But it is mankind who is king
of the Soviet lands,
the small man just born,
Ivan or Peter,
crying
calling for milk:
he, the heir.

Wide is the kingdom and soft
with tapestries of grass and snow,
its head, the summit
of the Ural Mountains,
barely covered by night's cold crown
while the sea licks the ice coastline
the sweet land,
glacial territories
or countries filled with grapes.
This land lacks nothing:
in motion
like a grand design
and from the time he is born

man owes it his song and his labor
the fertile kingdom, mankind's work.
Before this time darkness
lay across the land,
hunger and pain filling
time and space.
Then into history
strode Lenin
and changed the land,
then came Stalin
he changed mankind.
Then peace, war,
blood, wheat:
through great difficulty everything
came to fruition
with force and joy,
and today Ivan inherits
the red spring from sea to sea –
let me take you there by the hand.

Listen, listen to
this birdsong:
silver whistles in the wet tremor
of its matin voice,
I seek it among the needles
and pine parapets,
another song answering,
the forest peopled
with voices in the height.
From forest to forest they sing,
they share
from week to week,
dawn to dawn

trills just now born.
From village to village answering,
factory to factory,
river to river,
metal to metal,
song to song.

The vast kingdom sings,
and answers singing.
The leaves hold dew
in the clear morning.
The forest tastes
of fresh starlight.
Spring goes slowly
through the Russian land
as if crossing a planet,
fresh tendrils and men are born
beneath its silver feet.

2

Transiberian

I cross the Siberian autumn:
each birch a golden candelabra.
Suddenly a black tree, a red tree,
displays a wound or a blaze.
The steppe, the harsh vast face,
green breadth,
grain planet, earthy ocean.
I passed Novosibirsk by night,

founded by the new energy.
In the expanse its lights worked
in the midst of the night, new mankind
making nature new.
And you, great Yenisei River, you told me
with wide voice on passing, your word:
"No longer do my waters run in vain.
I am the blood of wakening life."

The small station where the rain
leaves a memory of water in the corners
and above the ancient, sweet wooden houses,
fragments of the forests,
have new guests, an iron
beam: they are the new tractors
that arrived yesterday, rigid, uniformed
soldiers of the land,
weapons of bread, an army
of peace and life.
Grain, wood, fruits of Siberia,
welcome
to the house of mankind:
no one gave you the right to be born,
no one knew you existed,
until the snow broke
and between the thaw's white wings
Soviet Man entered
to sow the seeds.
Oh Siberian lands,
at the yellow light
of the grandest autumn on Earth,
the golden leaves' joy,
all the light covers with its poured-out cup!

The Transiberian Railway
runs devouring the planet.
Every day an hour
yields before us,
falling beneath the train,
becoming a seed.
Alongside the Urals
we leave fall's good cold
and before Krasnoyarsk,
before a day,
invisible spring comes wearing
its tepid blue suit anew.
In the next cabin
a young geologist travels
with wife and small child.
Sakhalin Island waits for
them with forty shades
of cold and solitude,
but the metals also await
their date with the explorers.

Onward, Soviet child!
How shall we conquer solitude,
how shall we conquer the cold,
how shall we win peace,
unless you cross Siberia
and fill the islands?
The train branches off
all the way to Vladivostok
between steel-colored archipelagos
to the children who will change life,
who will transform cold
and solitude and wind

into flowers and metals.
Onward, children,
marching seven days
on the Transiberian Railway
to dream clear dreams of iron and harvests.

Onward, Transiberian train,
your tranquil will nearly circles the globe!
Vastness, broad land, running over it,
sliding on the train for days and days,
I loved your stepped latitudes,
your crops, your villages, your factories,
your men reducing you to matter
and your infinite autumn
that covered me with gold
while the train conquered
light and distance!

So will I lift my eyes to you,
Siberia, yellow
mother, vast
spring of the future!

3

Third love song to Stalingrad

Stalingrad with torrid wings
of summer, white
mansions rising:

a city like any other.
The people burdened
by their labor.
A dog crosses
the dusty day.
A girl runs
with a paper in her hand.
Nothing happens,
save the dark-watered Volga.
One by one from man's breast
houses rise –
and postage stamps,
mailboxes,
trees
all sprang to life,
children returned,
schools,
love returned,
mothers
gave birth once more,
cherries filled
branches,
sky-blown wind,
and then?

Yes, it's the same city,
no doubt.
The track was here,
the street,
the corner,
the meter and the centimeter
where our life and all
our life's meaning
was won

with blood.
Here we cut the knot
that squeezed history's
throat.
It was here. It seems a lie
that we now can
tread the street and see
the girl, the dog,
write a letter,
send a telegram,
but perhaps for this,
for this day the same
as every day,
for this simple sun
at peace with men
there was victory won,
here, in the ashes
of the holy land.

Today's bread, today's book,
a pine tree
planted just this morning,
a luminous street
newly arrived from the plans
where the engineer
traced it beneath the wind of war,
a young girl who passes, a dog
who crosses the dusty day,
oh miracles,
miracles of blood,
miracles of steel and the Party,
miracles of our new world.

Acacia branch with thorns and flowers,
where, where
will you hold stronger perfume
than in this place
where perfume was all erased,
where all fell
except the Soviet soldier,
the man of these days?

Oh scented branch,
here your scent
excels the gathered spring!

Here the aroma is mankind and hope,
here, acacia branch,
fire could not burn you
nor the wind of death bury you.
Here you were born each day
without ever having died,
and today in your scent the infinite person
of yesterday and tomorrow,
of the day after tomorrow,
returns to us to give his flowered eternity.
You are like a tractor factory:
today great metal flowers
flourish anew to till the land
multiplying seed.
The factory too
was ash,
twisted iron, smoke
bloodied by war,
but its heart was not stopped,
still learning to die and to be born again.

Stalingrad taught the world
life's lesson supreme:
be born, be born, be born,
and dying
it was born,
firing shots
it was born,
it fell flat and arose
with a ray in its hand.
All night it bled out
and yet in the dawn
it lent blood
to all Earth's cities.
The city turned pale in the black snow
all death falling
and when you looked
to see it fall, when we wept
its last bravery,
then she smiled on us,
Stalingrad
smiled on us.

And now
death has fled:
its only remnant a few broken walls,
contortion of iron
bombed out twisted,
just a trace
a proud scar,
the rest is clear, moon and space,
decision and whiteness,
and in the height
an acacia branch,

leaves, flowers, defending thorns,
the vast spring
of Stalingrad,
the invincible scent
of Stalingrad!

4

The Soviet angel

He was buried a hundred fifty years ago.
In silk and blood in St. Petersburg
he fell a filthy bullet
somewhere in his chest.
Time passed.
A hundred winter snows fell
over roofs and streets,
but still
the open bleeding
small red wound
in the stone chest, silk and gold
of St. Petersburg. A trickle
of blood accused. It came
and went,
rising through the cupolas,
running by the silk
of embroidered jackets,
at once it appeared
like a precious stone
above a belle's *dé*colleté,
and oh, it was just an accusing
clot of blood.

So it was,
so it was the blood of murdered
Pushkin
everywhere
an endless
thread.
In the silence
of St. Petersburg, in the stone and the water
of the sleeping city,
on the statue of Peter and his horse,
the thread,
the thread of blood
trickled and
trickled, seeking.

Then morn dawned one day
with shots firing.
A strange-textured tapestry
appeared
on the steps of the Winter Palace:
mankind and rage, hope and fire,
young heads and grey,
the face of the people
Lenin
with a blow
at the foot of hope
changed History.

Then
that thread of accusing blood
returned to its place
and clear, aerial and red,
the pensive angel

lived again.
Pushkin
gazed at his shirt:
the assassin's bullet
the filthy hole
no longer bled.
The people
expelled
gold-jacketed
swordsmen,
executioners with their medals of blood
and now
with the wound closed
and his head
graced by laurel wind
Pushkin started out upon the streets,
accompanying his people.

And so, alive again,
resplendent of stature,
waving in the sky
like a great banner,
mingling among the people
at the establishment's demise,
in the open country
with wet hair
or resting a bit
alongside wheat sheaves,
I saw young Pushkin.
My friend
did not speak,
one had to read him.
I traversed the vast geography
of the USSR,

watching him and reading him,
and he with his ancient voice
deciphered for me
lives and lands.
A calm pride,
like a dream,
overwhelmed his face
when at my side
he went flying
crystalline in the crystal air,
above the spacious liberty
of the cities and the plains.

5

On his death

Comrade Stalin,
I was by the sea on Isla Negra,
resting from battles and travels,
when word of your death arrived
like an ocean's blow.

First there was silence,
the stupor of things, and then
it crashed from the sea like a great wave
formed of seaweed, metals and men,
stones, foam and tears.
From history, time and space the wave
gathered his substance
and rose, crying above the world

until it came before me
to beat against my shore
and its mournful message
threw down my doors
with a great cry
as if of a sudden the world broke apart.

It was in 1914.
In the factories garbage and sorrows
piled up.
The rich men of the new century
sliced shares with their teeth
from oil and islands,
copper and canals.
No flag lifted its colors
without splashings of blood.
From Hong Kong to Chicago the police
sought documents and tried out
their machine guns on the people's flesh.
From dawn the military dispatches
ordered young soldiers to die.
In the *boîtes* of Paris filled with smoke
the gringos' dance was frenzied.
Mankind was bleeding to death.
A blood rain fell from the planet,
staining the stars.
Death tested its steel armor.
Hunger
in the streets of Europe
like a frozen wind threshing dry leaves
breaking bones.
Autumn blew across tattered rags.
War had stiffened the roads.
The smell of winter and blood

arose from Europe
as from an abandoned slaughterhouse.
All the while those who own
coal,
iron,
steel,
smoke,
banks,
gas,
gold,
flour,
nitrate,
the daily *El Mercurio*,
brothel owners,
North American senators,
filibusterers
laden with the gold and blood
of all nations,
they owned History too.
There they sat
in coat and tails, deeply occupied
awarding medals,
gifting themselves checks
at the entrances
and stealing them at the exits,
gifting themselves stocks
at the slaughterhouse
dividing into bite-sized
snippets the people and the world.

Then with modest
clothes and a worker's cap,
the wind came in,

the people's wind.
It was Lenin.
He changed the land, mankind, life.
Free revolutionary air
blew chaos through the stained
papers. A homeland was born
that has not ceased to grow.
It is as grand as the world, but with room
for even the heart of the
least
worker in factory, office,
farm or ship.
The Soviet Union.

Alongside Lenin
Stalin advanced
and so, with white shirt,
with grey worker's cap,
Stalin
with his calm pace,
entered History accompanied
by Lenin and the wind.
From then on Stalin
continued building. Everything
was in need. The czars left Lenin
cobwebs and tatters.
Lenin left the heritage
of a homeland free and broad.
Stalin peopled it
with schools and flour,
printing presses and apples.
Stalin thrust in his hand
from the Volga
to the snow

of the inaccessible North
and by his hand men
began to build.
Cities were born.
The deserts sang
for the first time with the voice of water.
Minerals
were mined
leaving
their dark dreams,
ascending
they made rails, wheels,
locomotives, threads bearing electric syllables
across all distance and expanse.
Stalin built.
From his hands
were born
grains,
tractors,
teaching,
roads,
and there he is,
a plain man like you and like me,
should you and I succeed in being
plain like him.
But we will learn.
His simplicity and his wisdom
in the form of generous bread
and unbendable steel
helps us to be men each day,
each day helping us to be men.

To be men! This is
the Stalinist law!
It is difficult to be a communist.
One must learn to be one.
To be communist men
is even harder,
and it is necessary to learn from Stalin
his serene intensity,
his concrete clarity,
his disdain
for empty glitter,
for hollow editorial abstraction.
He went straightaway to
disentangling the knot,
showing true doctrinal clarity,
dealing with problems
without sentences hiding
emptiness,
right to the weak center
that we will put right through our battle
pruning the foliage
opening the way for the fruit to grow.
Stalin is midday,
the maturity of mankind and the people.
In the war
the burning cities
saw him
extract hope
from the rubble,
recast it anew,
and attack with his lightning
destroying
the fortress of darkness.

But he also aided the apple trees
of Siberia
to yield their fruit
in the face of the tempest.
He taught all
to grow, to grow,
plants and metals,
creatures and rivers
he taught them all to grow,
to yield fruit and fire.
He taught them Peace
and so held back
with his outspread chest
the wolves of war.

Stalinists. We bear this name with pride.
Stalinists. This is the hierarchy of our time!
Workers, fishermen, Stalinist musicians!
Steel smiths, copper fathers, Stalinists!
Doctors, nitrate miners, Stalinist poets!
Professors, students, Stalinist peasants!
Laborers, employees, Stalinist women,
hail to you this day!
The daylight has not disappeared,
the fire has not left,
but rather light, bread, fire and hope
all increase
in the invincible Stalinist era!

In his last days the dove, Peace,
the wandering persecuted rose,
alit on Stalin's shoulders, and the giant
lifted it to his forehead's height.

So the distant peoples saw peace.
From steppes and seas, plains, assemblies,
men's eyes turned
their gaze to this beacon with doves,
and neither the brutal rancor
nor the haughty venom
of the bloodthirsty, nor the wry grimace
of Churchill or Eisenhower or Trujillo,
nor the widespread barking of the sellouts,
nor the defeated jackal's guttural growl,
diminished his epic stature
or stained his simple strength.
Facing the sea on Isla Negra I spied
at half-mast Chile's flag in the dawn.
The coast was lonely
and a silver cloud was mixed
with the ocean's solemn foam.
In the midst of its mast, in its blue field,
my homeland's single star
seemed a tear between sky and land.
A villager passed by, greeted me,
understanding,
and took off his hat.
A boy came by and gave me his hand.

Later the sea-urchin fisherman,
the old diver and poet, Gonzalo,
approached to accompany me beneath the flag.
"He was the wisest of all men,"
he said looking at the sea with his old eyes,
with the old eyes of the people.

And then for a long time
we said nothing to one another.

A wave crashed on the shore's stones.
"But now Malenkov will carry on his work,"
continued the poor worn-jacketed fisherman
lifting himself up.
I looked at him surprised, thinking:
How, how does he know that?
Where did he learn it, on this solitary coast?
Then I understood the sea had taught him.

And so we mourned together, a poet,
a fisherman and the sea
for the distant Captain who on entering death
left to all people, as a heritage, his life.

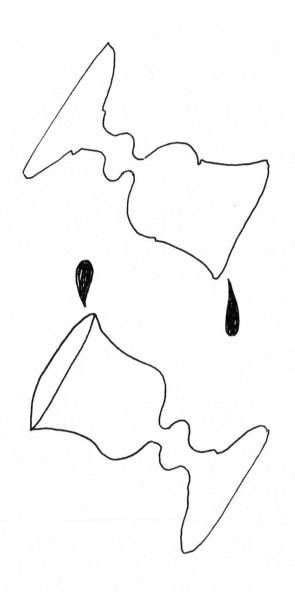

VII

LAND OF THE GRAPE CLUSTER

1

The green tunic

I walked
on mountain roads,
their green-tunic vines enveloped me,
I tasted wine and water,
Italy's crops –
fine flour blowing
across my hands, olive oil slipping through,
the land's riches.
I walked
by the factories
I spoke with your workers
I know the white
smile on their blackened faces,

that smile like firm flour,
its mill rough soil.
I walked
among your fishermen in the islands,
I know the lonely song
of a man alone in stony solitude,
I have hauled fishnets,
and gazed on charred hillsides
in the South, scraping the innards
of the poorest land.
And I have seen
where Benedetti, guerrillero, my friend,
immobile with bomb in hand
left there forever
his face but not his smile.
Everywhere
I touched
human flesh
contact
for me like fertile soil.
In the past I walked
speaking with suits,
greeting hats,
giving my hand to gloves,
walking among men without man,
women without woman,
houses without doors.
Italy, you weigh everyman's measure
as the grain man does wheat,
amassing kernels,
pure caudal treasure,
deep sowing of delicacy and hope.
In the mornings
the oldest of the

women, olive-colored gray,
brought me rock flowers, roses plucked
from the harsh hillside ridge.
Roses and green oil, these were the gifts
I collected, but
above all the
wisdom and song
I learned from your islands.
And so will I carry in my hands
wherever I go –
as if it were the touch
of pure wood,
musical and fragrant
guarded by my fingers –
the people's pace
their voice and substance
battle and smile
roses and oil
the land, the water, the wine
of your land and your people.
I did not dwell in
temples with their friezes
fallen with ancient rulers
nor among their broken statues,
nor did I live by lapis and perfume alone,
but I endured the deepest shudders
of mankind's ocean:
there in the worst misery
of dismantled slums
I set my heart
like a nighttime net,
and I know children's
tears and hunger,

but
I also know the union's step
and victory.
I did not allow my breast
to dissolve in sweetness
like an untouched lyre,
but rather walked through the factories
and I know the face
of Italy will change.
I touched at last
the depth
of tomorrow's unceasing seeding,
and I hope.
And I bathed myself in the waters
of an eternal spring.

2

Tresses of Capri

Capri, stone queen,
I lived in stages of
joy and pain,
your clothing
the color of amaranth and lily,
the vineyard full
of radiant clusters
I won in the land,
a quivering treasure
of perfume and hair,
Midday lamp, extended rose,

my planet's honeycomb.
I disembarked in winter.
The island's base guarded
its sapphire suit
and naked robed in mist
emerges like a maritime cathedral.
Stone is the beauty of Capri.
The pure springtime hiding treasures
in the rock fissures,
each fragment of her skin
coming back to life.
A red and yellow lightning bolt
beneath the thin light lay asleep
awaiting the moment
its power to unchain.
By the shore of flightless birds,
in the midst of the sky,
a hoarse cry, wind
and inexpressible foam.
Your garments silver and stone,
scarcely the blue flower bursts
embroidering a hirsute mantel
with celestial blood.
Oh solitude of Capri,
silver grape wine,
winter cup, full
of invisible labor,
I lifted your firm frame,
your delicate light, your forms,
your star-brightened liquor
drinking as if life were
being born in me.
Island, from your walls I detached

the small nocturnal
flower guarding it in my breast.
And from the sea your girth surrounding
I fashioned a ring of water
that remained there among the waves,
encircling the proud towers
of flourishing stone,
the craggy summits
that sustained my love,
they will protect with implacable hands
the trace of my kisses.

3

The police

We are the police.
 "And you? Who are you?
Where are you from, where
are you trying to go?
Your father? Your brother-in-law?
Who did you sleep with the past seven nights?"
"I slept with my lover, I am perhaps,
perhaps, perhaps, I am Poetry."
And so a gondola
blacker than the others
ferried them behind me in Venice,
in Bologna at night,
on the train: I am a wandering shadow
followed by shadows.
In Venice I saw the upright Campanile

lifting up among the doves of San Marcos
the three-cornered hat of the police.
And Paulina, naked, in the museum,
when I kissed her cold and lovely mouth
said: "Are your papers in order?"

There are inquisitions in Dante's house
beneath the old Florentine ceilings,
and David
with his marble eyes, without pupils
forgot his father, Buonarroti,
because each day they made him recount
what his blind eyes had seen.
Nevertheless that day
when they took me to the Swiss border
the police quickly found
themselves faced off by
militant poetry.
I will not forget the Roman crowd
in the station who, at night,
plucked me from the hands
of the pursuing police.

How to forget Guttuso's guerilla gesture
the face of Giuliano,
the wave of wrath, the blow upon the noses
of the bloodhounds, how to forget Mario,
from whom in exile
I learned to love Italy's freedom,
and now I spied his furious white head
blending into the choppy sea
of my friends and my enemies?
I will not forget Elsa Morante's

little umbrella
falling on a policeman's chest
like a weighty petal filled with florid strength.
And so in Italy
by the people's will,
heavy with poetry,
united strength,
tender action,
my destiny remained.

And so it was
as this book was born
surrounded by the sea and lemon trees,
listening in silence,
behind the wall of the police,
as it fought and fights,
as it sang and sings
the valiant people
who won the battle that I might
rest on the island that awaited me
with a flowering jasmine branch in its mouth
and in its small hands the source of my song.

4

The tattered gods

Misery has lived for centuries
in Southern Italy. See her throne:
the trembling black spider webs
hang from it like tapestries

and grey rats gnaw on the
ancient wood.
Hole-pierced throne that through
the broken windows
of the Naples night breaths
with a terrible death rattle,
and between the holes
black curls fall on the temples
of handsome boys
like little tattered gods.
Oh Italy, who lives in your dwelling
of marble and splendor?
Is that how, old red she-wolf,
you treat your golden progeny?
Sad upon the roads is the voice of the South.
The sky lets fall
a sour shade on broken houses,
doors emit
the tangled branch
of hunger and poverty
and nonetheless
your loud-echoing head sings on.
Sad upon the roads is the voice of the South.
The villages hold out
more than one hungry mouth
and yet sing.
I drink the red wine
raising in the cup
not only the ripe sun,
but wrath's ancient light.

Italy's peasants
march toward the land.

They grew weary
of scraping the stone
and submitted to dominion,
to feudal domain.
Men, women, children
now gathered together beneath a tree
and set themselves to
cleanse the land,
to dig it,
to till it,
and wheat falls
in the furrow,
the hands of the poor clutched
the fistful of wheat
as if it were gold,
and then
the first kitchen casting smoke,
fire,
clothes washed,
life.

Soldiers came,
the Christian state.
"You may not sow,
you may not light a fire.
The owners'
land
must lay fallow.
Root up the wheat,
fill in the furrow,
quench the fire."
The old faces,
the wrinkled hands,

so like the land, furrows, seeds, fire,
remained immobile
yet they sang when the soldiers
lifted their rifles,
and they fell singing.

Blood watered the wheat
but there grows
invincible grain,
grain that sings unto death.
This happened while I lived in Italy.
And that's how the peasants
conquered the land.

5

The fleet arrives

When the North American fleet
arrives
Italy's pastoral flag
vanishes.
Did the sky disappear,
and where are the guitars?
That wave of honey and light
that envelops
people, conversations, monuments,
everything hides, leaving only
the steel presence in the bay,
slow reptiles,
the cursed tongues of war,

and on high
the invader's flag
with prison stripes
and stolen stars.
Brothels
flourish,
and there jolting and jolting
the civilizing sailors
cross, demolish the shoreline homes
of the poor
as they enter with fist blows
just as happened
before in Havana,
Panama, Valparaiso,
Nicaragua, Mexico.
Following the fleet
a land caravan comes
in trains and trucks the whores
preceding them to the next port
where their grey ships go
defending culture.
Ay, what hardships they suffer – not
enough port hotels for
the girls to lie in wait!
Ah but for this
the whole government has mobilized itself.
Signor Gasperi runs dressed
in his gravest jacket,
and the Prefect of Police himself
sweeps the dormitories
with great efficiency.
Italy's senior ministers meet,
congratulating themselves
and the City Council President

funereal and gaunt as death's casket
intones with a smooth voice:
"Overcoming hardships
we have complied with our duties
to the North American fleet.
Moreover, I can tell you with pride
that this afternoon,
I barred a show of paintings,
cast out a dangerous poet
and sent the Leningrad Ballet packing.
Thus do we Italians show how
we defend Catholic culture."
Meanwhile in the ports
the pastoral flag hides itself,
the light of Italy
hides itself,
and the battle ships' shadow
sleeps upon the water, just as
reptiles crouch in putrid ponds
of the jungle.
Nevertheless
the Italian sky is blue
her poor land generous
her people's heart wide
their stature valiant
and what I tell you is true –
but it won't last forever.

6

Singing I built you

I created you, invented you in Italy.
I was alone.
The sea between the fissures
unleashed with violence
its seminal foam.
So ragged spring
prepared itself,
sleeping sprouts half-opened
wet stalks,
a secret thirst and blood
wounded my head.
I built you singing
from sea and the land.
I needed your mouth, the pure arch
of your small foot, your hair
of burnt grain.
I called you and you came from the night,
and in the half-opened light of dawn
I found that you existed
and that from me as from the sea foam
you were born, my little goddess.
First you were a seed laid low
waiting
beneath the dark soil
its springtime growth,
and I asleep then
sensed your touch
beneath the ground,

because you were ready to be born,
and I had sown you
within my being. Then time
and forgetfulness came
and I forgot you were with me
growing alone
inside of me, and suddenly
I found that your mouth
had arisen from the earth
like a giant flower.
It was you who existed.
I had created you.
My heart then
shivered recognizing
and sought to deny you.
But no, we could not.

The land was full
of sacred grape clusters.
Sea and land in your hands
burst open with the ripe gifts.
And so your sweetness was poured out
in my breath and in my senses
because you were created by me
to help me live joy.
And so you were the land,
the flower and the fruit,
so from the sea you came
submerged waiting
and you stretched yourself by me
in the dream
from which we do not awake.

VIII

FAR AWAY, IN THE DESERTS

1

Earth and sky

Suddenly I saw my homeland
in the heights of Mongolia,
desert heights:
the Great North, Chile,
dry skin, scratched from the land
at the limits of the sky.
I saw the sand mountains,
the quiet expanse:
I grew still listening to
the Gobi's cruel wind,
storms
in the "roof of the world"
all so much like
my Andean home,

land of copper, salt and sky.
And soon the wind
carried a camel's scent,
a burnt trace became incense,
the light held
a finger
above the silk
of a red banner,
and I saw that I was far
from my homeland.
The Mongols were no longer
the wandering
horsemen
of the wind and the sand:
they were my comrades.
The showed me
their laboratories.

Metallurgy – that sweet word
in the heights above:
there where magicians
wove wisdom and spider webs,
in Durga, black Durga,
now a new name
shines –
Ulan Bator,
people's captain.

And everything
was so simple.
Young university men,
students from the desert,
bent
over microscopes.

In the cold sands
of the highlands where
new institutes
shone,
mines were drilled,
books and music
sang in the
wind chorus
mankind was reborn.

2

My brother was there

There I was.
There I've seen
not only sand and air,
not only
camels and metals,
but mankind,
my distant
brothers,
born now in the midst
of planetary solitude,
differentiating themselves
from Nature,
understanding
the mystery
of electricity and life,
giving their hands to the East

and the West,
giving hands to the sky
and the land, dividing,
existing,
assuring
bread and tenderness
among their children.

Oh harsh lands,
lunar buttresses,
from you
ascends
the seed
of the socialist era
and flower and beauty
climb
from the stone,
the factory that speaks to the sky
with smoke words
and minerals mastered
now fashions tools and joy.

3

But it yielded fruit

But when
between the arid
summit ranges
a man appeared,
transformed,
when from the yurt

a man came
to battle Nature,
a man not only
from a tribe,
but from the ardent human mass,
not an errant
fugitive of solitary heights,
sand horseman,
but my comrade,
linked to the destiny
of his people,
showing solidarity
with all human breath,
son and heir of hope,
then,
the task was finished
between the mountains' scars:
there too the man became our brother.

There the harsh land yielded its fruit.

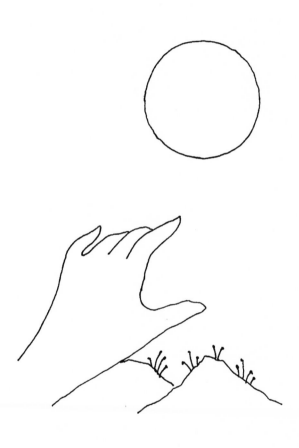

IX

THE BROKEN CAPITAL

1

In these years

Now
in these years
after mid-century
a timorous silence
trembles
from the West, startled.
Again, again
perhaps war.

The cold map
crossed by cypresses,
vertical shadows,
the night traversed
by dagger or lightning.

And so the threat
above roof and bread.
Silence
of the black-leaved tree,
the shadow
covers Greece.
Again bitter water
above the radiant age
of blind statues.

What is happening?
Where are we?
Some time ago a king and a queen
were prefabricated,
"made in England."
So this is the history
of this terrible time,
cruel officials
resurrected
from the bloody opera,
the North Americans
who administer
the rose
of Praxiteles
razing
with this and with that.
Who would have thought,
who
would have dared
to think that the purest stones,
cut with dawn's thread,
would be splattered,
that Greece would fall
into a black Chicago pit.

Who would say it
but the Greek stars,
the lines of the tragic muse
of the most ancient time,
and so it was happening.
The zooming bees
fashion
honey with blood,
light from martyrdom,
cells
of outraged architecture.

2

A Glance at Greece

Oh tears, it isn't time
to stream from my eyes,
it isn't the hour
to stream from men's eyes,
eyelids, lift yourselves
from sleep's darkness, clear
or shaded pupils,
tearless eyes, look to Greece
crucified on its own wood.
Watch her the whole
night, year, day,
pouring out her people's blood,
beating her temples
upon her terrible thorned capitals.
See, eyes of the world,

what pure Greece bears,
the slave trader's lash,
and so by night and year
and month and day
see how the head
of her proud people is raised.
From each drop
fallen in martyrdom,
mankind grows anew,
thought weaves his banners,
action strengthens the castle height
stone to stone
and hand to hand.

Oh bright Greece,
if darkness spilled its sack
of black stars into you, you know
that clarity lies within you,
that you gather
the whole night in your lap
until from your hands
dawn rises,
white, flying, wet with dew.
By its light we will see you smile,
ancient bright mother of men,
victorious,
showing us your white figure
afresh between the mountains.

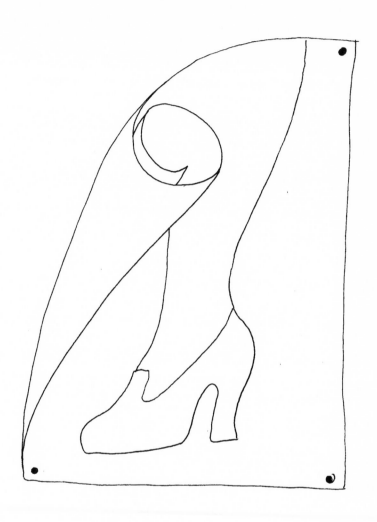

X

DIVIDED BLOOD

1

Morning in Berlin

I awoke. It was Berlin.
Through the window
I saw the toothless heart,
the crazed tomb,
the ash,
the heaviest ruins,
with fluting and friezes
damaged,
balconies twisted into a black jaw,
walls now lost, missing
their windows, their doors,
their men, their women,
and inside a mountain
of piled rubble,

suffering and arrogance mingled
in doom's flour, death's mill.

Oh citadel, oh blood
needlessly vanished,
And maybe this is, this is
your first victory,
even among black rubble
the peace you have known,
cleansing the ashes and lifting
your fortress toward all men,
taking from your ruins
not the dead
but common man,
new man,
that he might build buildings
of love and peace and life.

2

Young Germans

As a red branch
appears in a burnt tree
and in it
time's flower shines
so, Germany, in your face
burnt by war
your new youth enlightens
the burns and the scars of the past Hell.
Arriving by train

from Bohemia
I greeted today's flourishing youth
along the Elba
by its ancient and translucent course,
their strong smiles
hands
full of flowers for me
boys and girls
laden with lilies.
But it was not only the flowers
shedding light above the water,
it was the new-blossoming being,
the smile snatched from a cherry tree,
the direct gaze,
the strong hands that squeezed yours,
and the eyes pointedly blue.
There the land shook
with all cruelty and punishment
and now,
youths reborn
from water and land,
flowers in their mouths,
lifting love above the land,
the word Stalin
on millions of lips,
flourishing.
Oh wonder!
here is new life,
tree of light, hive,
endless granary,
peace and life,
branch and branch,
water and water,

grape cluster with grape cluster,
from vanquished scars
to newly ripened dawn.

And I forgot the ruins,
the burnt stone's runes,
the fire's lesson,
I forgot the war,
I forgot the hate,
because I saw life.
Oh youth,
German youth,
your spring's new guardians,
strong frank youth of new Germany,
look to the East,
look to the vast Union
of beloved Republics.
See too how from her ruins
a strong smile
dawns in Poland.
Giant China has shaken loose
her chains filled with blood
and is now our unbounded sister.

Before you
lies the world's treasure,
not ancient looted treasure,
but new treasure,
the broad space full
of fraternal people,
peace, spring wind, meeting
a stranger from abroad
not come to rob us.
We guard a steel thread

as it passes through
and grows everywhere,
the sea singing beside us
its eternal foam hymn,
and like a daily telegram the air
leaves us news.
How many new factories have been born,
how many schools have erased the shadow,
how many children from now on know
the hidden language
of metals and stars,
how we take bread from the earth
for all
and give fresh life to the land,
old mother of all mankind.
We shall create new water,
heavenly rice,
crystal motors.
We shall extend
space beyond the islands.
In the deserts of fire and sand
we see how spring dances in our arms,
because nothing will be forgotten,
not the land,
not mankind.
Mankind will not be forgotten
and this is treasure indeed.
You young men who in the depths
of war
held a smile
that will not be smothered,
this is treasure indeed:
not to forget mankind.

Because so it is that the Earth is greater
than all stars together.
So we grow each day and each
day are richer in mankind,
we have more brothers,
in the air,
in the mines,
in the high plains of metallic Mongolia.
Mankind,
to the East, to the North, to the South,
to the West, even above,
where the wind walks,
mankind.
See son, how they hail you,
see how your family has grown,
how great is the land and it's yours,
how great is the land and it's mine –
it is for everyone,
greet,
greet the world,
the new world that has been born
and will grow with you
because you are the seed.

You will grow, we shall grow.
And now no one can fell the tree
or cut its roots
because in your heart they are growing
and the tree will fill the whole world
with flowers and songs and fruit.

3

The wounded city

Berlin cutoff
continued bleeding
secret blood while the dark
night came and went.
Time's brilliance
like a lightning bolt in East Berlin
lightened the step
of the free young men
who lifted the city again.
In the darkness I passed
from side to side
and the sadness of an ancient age
filled my heart as a spade
laden with filth.
In Berlin the West guarded
its unchaste "Liberty,"
and here as well
the statue with her false
beacon, her gross and leprous mask
painted with alcohol-ridden
carmine lipstick,
and in her hand a garrote
newly arrived from Chicago.
West Berlin,
with your market
of young whores
and drunk invading soldiers,
West Berlin,

You've postered the walls
with obscene legs,
half-naked vampires
all to sell your pitiful goods,
and even the cigarettes have the taste
of black vice.
Pedophiles dance squeezing
State Department experts.
Lesbians found
their protected paradise
and their saint: Saint Ridgway.
West Berlin,
you are a pustulant sore
on Europe's ancient face,
the old Nazi foxes
slide on the snot
of your filthy bright-lit lanes,
and Coca-Cola and anti-Semitism
run freely
over your shit and ruins.

It is a cursed city,
daughter of tortoise
Truman and the exhumed
Hitlerian crocodile,
they file down its teeth,
and shaft it with bayonets
while the *boogie-woogie*
loosens the threads
of the soldiers' sex trade.
"Young German girl
in the 19th springtime of her life
seeks older man, or established
businessman, to buy

her youth," says the newspaper.
And in the night's dreadful
shadow
tanks disembark.
The gases that murdered
half of Europe
return to operation
with a North American monopoly.
Old Nazi killers
stroll about anew and bark
in the cafes, sniffing out blood.
Abstract art and the conflict of the "soul"
are the artistic themes, splattered
with blood and sex,
while as in the good old days of Adolf
they shut down newspapers
and beat the womb
of any communist girl
who spits in their face.

Such is life,
and in this Berlin men fall
in every cluster of death.
For this black city,
pustulous, poisonous,
liberty opened her main veins,
bleeding out from the Volga
to the black waters of the Spree.
For this North American dance
and this Washington cudgeling
they fought, ay, all men fought
from one sea to another,
to every land and island.

Therefore I flee stride upon stride
to East Berlin, where the night also
covers the broken roofs,
but I see the dream,
I know that labor sleeps
at night to gather its strength.
I see the last youths who sing
returning from the factories.
I see the light through the night,
the color of the flowers
that filled the trains when I arrived in Germany.
I breathe because here mankind
is my brother.
Here they do not coddle the wolf,
here they do not file down teeth
to unbridle the hunt.
Here is the smell
of a school swept and cleaned,
the smell of newly-carried bricks,
the smell of fresh water,
the smell of a bakery,
the smell of truth and wind.

XI

HOMESICKNESS AND RETURN

Intermission

1

Returnings

In Southern Italy, on the island,
just arrived
from dazzling Hungary, from cragged
Mongolia,
the sun over the winter,
the sun over the sea of the winter.
Again,
again we begin,
my love, let us draw again
a circle on a star.
Let there be light,
let there be clarity.

Let us draw
a circle on the bread.
Let all goods be shared
among all mankind.
Let justice be done,
we will do it.

Life,
you gave me
everything.
You took loneliness away from me,
the lonely light
and the wall.
You gave me
love in full hands,
battles,
joys,
all.
And you gave it to me
in spite of myself.
I closed my eyes.
I didn't wish to see it.
You came
despite all that,
complete,
complete with all your gifts
and with the wound that I myself gave you
like a bloody flower
that made me stagger but not fall.

2

The traveler from Capri

Where, plant or beam of light,
where, black beam or tough plant,
where have you come from
now to reach this corner of the sea?

The farthest continent's shadow
is in your eyes, an open moon
in your wild mouth,
and your face is the eyelid of a sleeping fruit.
Your frame the silken tip of a star,
your lips hold the blood and fire
of ancient lances.

Where did you seize
a spring's limpid petals from,
where did you carry the seed to,
the seed I recognize? And so
the Capri sea is in you, strange sea,
behind you the boulders, the olive oil,
the just and well-formed clarity,
but you, you I know,
I know that rose,
I know the blood of that rose,
I know that I know it,
I know where it came from,
and I smell the free air your presence brings
to my memory, scent of rivers and horses.
Your long hair is a red cart

filled with quick kisses and news,
your "yes" and your clarion call
speak to me at midday,
at midnight they call at my door
as if they divined
how to retrace my steps.

Perhaps, unknown,
the salt of Maracaibo
sounds in your voice filling it with slumber,
or the cold wind of Valparaiso
shook your reason when you were growing up.
The truth is that today, watching you pass
between the rose-breasted birds
of the headlands of Capri,
the blaze of your eyes, something
I saw fly from your breast, the air
circling your skin, nocturnal light
exuding from your heart,
something came to my mouth
with a taste of the flower I used to know,
something daubed my lips with the dark liquor
of my childhood's wild herbs,
and I thought: That woman,
even though the blue dome should spill all
the clusters of the sky into her throat,
even though behind her the temples
made halos with their crowned whiteness
so beautiful,
she is not, she is another,
something sizzling in her calls me:
all the land that gave me life
is in her gaze, those fragile
hands grasping water from the hillside slope,

those tiny feet traversing
my country's volcanic isles.

Oh you, unknown to me, sweet and firm,
when now your footstep
descends until lost,
and only the columns
of the broken temple and the sea's green
sapphire that sings in my exile
remain alone, alone
with me and with your shadow,
my heart gave out a great beat,
as if a great stone suspended
in the invisible height
should suddenly fall
above the water and make foam to leap.

And I awoke from your presence then
with my face soaked by your splashing,
water and perfume and dream,
distance and land and wave!

3

When, Chile?

Chile,
long petal
of sea and wine and snow,
when,
oh when,
and when
I am with you again
You'll cinch your belt
white foam and black around my waist,
and I will loose my poetry
over your land.

There are men
half-fish, half-wind,
there are other men made of water.
I am of the soil.
I wander through the world
each time with greater joy:
each city gives me new life.
The world is being born.
But if it rains in Lota
it rains on me,
if in Lonquimay the snow
slips from the leaves
the snow falls wherever I am.
Cautin's dark wheat grows inside me.
I have a tall pine tree in Villarrica,
I have sand in the Great North,

I have a golden rose in the countryside,
and the wind that tumbles
the last wave of Valparaiso
beats upon my chest
with hollowed sound
as if there my heart
had a broken window.

The month of October came
so quickly after the last October
that when it arrived it was as though
I gazed on motionless time.
Here it is autumn. I cross
the Siberian steppe.
Day after day all is yellow,
the tree and the factory,
the land and what the new man
creates in her: gold and red flame,
an immense tomorrow, snow, purity.
In my country spring
comes from the North to the South
fragrant as a young girl
by the black stones of Coquimbo,
by the surf's solemn shore
flying with unshod feet
toward the wounded isles.
Filling me you offer
not just springtime and land.
I am not a solitary man –
I was born in the South.
From the frontier I brought with me
the loneliness and
gallop of the last caudillo.

The Party made me dismount
and I become a man, and I walked
the beaches and the mountain ranges
loving and discovering.

My people, is it true that in the spring
my name sounds on your ears
and you sense me
as if I were a river
passing by your door?

I am a river. If you listen
carefully beneath the salt mines
of Antofagasta, or even
in the South by Osorno
or toward the cordillera, in Melipilla,
or in Temuco, in the night
wet with stars and sounding laurel,
put your ears to the ground,
you'll hear me coursing by,
submerged, singing.

October, oh spring,
return me to my people.
How can I bear not to see
your thousand men,
your thousand girls,
to carry part of their hope
upon my shoulders?

How can I live and not march with the flag
that comes to my hands
passed hand to hand through the ranks
of our great struggle?

Oh Patria, Patria,
oh Patria, when
oh when and when,
when shall I be with you?

Far from you
I am but half-land, half-man,
and today once again spring passes.
I fill myself with your flowers,
with your victory on my forehead,
my roots remain in you.

Oh when
I see your fierce spring,
and walk in my worn shoes
with all your sons
through fields and streets.
Oh when
I go with Elías Lafferte
through the whole golden prairie.
Oh when with wandering lips
I press your mouth,
you, Chilena, waiting for me.
Oh when
I enter the Party's meeting hall
and sit down beside Pedro Fogonero,
whom I do not know and yet
is more my brother than my brother.
Oh when the green thunder of your sea mantle
shakes me from this dream.
Oh when, Patria, I go electioneering
from house to house gathering frail freedom

to shout in the midst of the street.
Oh when, Patria, you marry me
with sea-green eyes
and gown of snow
we will have millions of new children
who will return the Earth to the hungry.

Oh Patria, without rags,
oh my spring,
oh when
oh when and when
I awake in your arms
drenched with sea and dew.
Oh when I am near
you I will circle your waist,
no one will touch you,
I will defend you
singing,
when
I go with you, when
you go with me, when
oh when.

4

The belt from Orinoco

Carlos Augusto sent me a leather belt
from Orinoco.

Now I wear
a river at my waist,
nuptial birds who in their flight lift
petals from the thicket,
broad thunder lost in my childhood
today I wear it tied about me,
sewn with lightning bolts and rain,
fastening together my old trousers.
Seaboard leather, river leather,
I love you and I touch you,
you are flower and wood,
lizard and mud,
you are the vastness of clay.
I run my hand over your ridges
as though over my country.
You have the lips
of a kiss that seeks me.
But it's not just love you have, oh land,
for I know you guard as well
the tooth mark, the blade, the exile –
they ask for me every day.
Your coast, America,
holds not just feathers
of a burning fan,
not just bright sugar,

flickering fruit,
but also the poisonous whisper
of the secret stab wound.

Here on my own
I've tried the river on myself:
it girds my waist well.
The Orinoco
is like a missing last name.
My name is Orinoco,
I must go with the water at my waist,
and from now on
that leather line
will grow with the moon,
will open its estuaries at dawn,
will walk with me in the streets
will enter the meetings with me
reminding me
where I come from:
from the rugged lands
of Sinaloa and Magallanes,
from peaks of Andean iron,
from hurricane-blown islands,
but more than all those places,
from the Orinoco,
green crocodile river,
wrapped by its breathing,
between its two banks always newly drawn
spreading its song throughout the land.

Carlos Augusto, thanks,
young brother, for in my exile
you sent me homeland's water.
One day you will see our people's face

appear in the river's
current running free,
uniting us,
high and happy singing with the waters.
And when that face looks upon us
we will think "we did our part"
and we will sing with our rivers,
with our people we will sing.

5

One day

To you, my love,
I consecrate this day.
It was born blue, with a white
wing in the midst of the sky.
Light falls
upon still cypresses.
From a leaf by the shore
or a spot of sun on stone
tiny creatures crawled.
The day stays blue
until entering night like a river
and makes the shadows tremble
with its blue waters.
To you, my love, this day.

I sensed it from afar,
still dreaming,

scarcely touching
its endless woven net
and thought: this is for her.
It was a silver heartbeat,
a blue fish flying over the sea,
the touch of dazzling sand,
an arrow's flight
between Heaven and Earth
piercing my blood
like a beam cradling my body
with bursting daylight clear.

It is for you, my love.

I said: it is for her.
This dress is hers.
Blue lightning suspending itself
above water and earth
I consecrate to you.

To you, my love, this day.

Lift this day with your hands:
like an electric goblet
or a corolla of quivering water,
drink it with your eyes and mouth,
pour it in your veins
that the same light may
burn in your blood and mine.

And I give you this day
with all it brings:
clear sapphire grapes and
a broken gust of wind

that bears to your window
the sorrows of the world.

I give you the whole day.
We will make our life's bread
of clarity and pain,
without rejecting what the wind brings us
nor accepting only Heaven's light,
but the bitter marks of Earth's shadow.

It all belongs to you.
This whole day with its blue cluster
and the secret tear of blood
you find in the soil.

And the darkness will not blind you
nor the dazzling light:
live are made
from this human dough
 and so we eat the bread of mankind.

And our love forged in dim light
and brilliant shadow
will be as this conquering day
entering like a clear river at midnight.

Take this day, beloved.
This whole day is yours.

I give it to your eyes, my love,
I give it to your breast,
I give it in your hands and your hair,
like a celestial branch.

I give it to you
that you might make of it
a gown
of blue silver and water.
When the night comes
flooded by this day
with tremulous net,
stretch out beside me,
touch me and cover me
with all starred weavings
of light and shadow,
then close your eyes
that I may sleep.

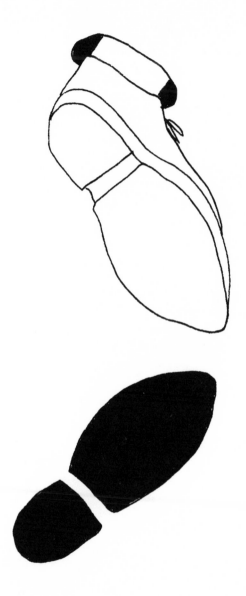

XII

THE SILK FLOWER

1

The distant book

Korea, your home
was a vibrant garden
of new flowers building themselves.
Your silk peace was
a green shawl,
a lily that lifted
its yellow lightning flash.

From Asia you gathered
exhumed light.
You wove
with ancient threads
new weft, new cloth.
Your bloodied doll's dress
changed to factory jeans

and silk threads
gathered treasure from the cascades,
carried words into the wind.

You wished
to cut out your own star
with your hands
and place it
in the frame of the firmament.

2

The invaders

They came.

They who before had leveled
Nicaragua.

They who stole Texas.

They who shamed Valparaiso.

They who with filthy claws
strangle the throat
of Puerto Rico.

They landed in Korea.

They arrived.

With napalm and dollars,
destruction, blood,
ashes, tears.

With death.

They came.

Mother and child
they burned alive in the village.

They poured burning petrol
on the flowering school.

Destroying lives and life.

Seeking from the air
even the very last
shepherd on the mountains
to kill him.

To lop off the breasts
of the shining guerrillera.

To slay prisoners in their beds.

They arrived.

With their bars and their stars.
And their murdering planes.

They arrived.

And suddenly
there was nothing but death.
Smoke, ashes, blood, death.

3

Hope

In every age mankind
bears witness.
It seems that the seeds and the lamps
were quickly snuffed out
but that isn't true.
A man
appears then,
a nation, a flag,
a flag we didn't know,
and above the flag pole
and the rippling color,
higher than the blood,
light lived again among mankind
and the seed returned to be sown.
Honor to you, Korea,
mother of our age,
our mother of ruined lips,
our mother cut down in martyrdom,
mother burned in every village,
ash mother,
wasteland mother,
homeland mother!

4

Your blood

Yes, we know,
yes, we know the whole story.
Your dead sons and daughters
we counted them
one by one each long night.
There is no number nor is there name
for such sorrows,
but neither is there a number
for what you gave us,
for the bleeding
heroes who in that hour
placed in your hands,
Korea,
the proud treasure,
freedom, not only
your freedom, Korea,
but all freedom,
everyone's,
mankind's freedom.

5

The peace we owe you

To your blood, Korea,
defender
of flowers,
the world owes its peace.

With your blood, Korea,
with your tragic severed hand,
you defended us all!

With your blood, Korea,
in my time, in these hard years,
freedom could speak your name
and sustain your heritage.

The lamps
will stay lit
and the seeds will seek the earth.

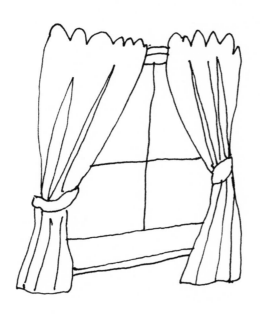

XIII

PASSING THROUGH THE FOG

1

London

In the deep night, London,
barely glimpsed,
innumerable eyes,
harsh hidden shadows,
stores filled with chairs,
chairs and chairs, chairs.
The black sky
seated over London,
over its black fog,
shoes and shoes,
river and river,
streets ground down by the teeth
of iron-colored misery,
and beneath the garbage
the poet Eliot
in his old tailcoat

reading to the maggots.
They asked me when
had I been born, why had I come
to disturb the Empire.
It was all police
with books and machine guns.
They asked
about my grandfather
and my uncles,
about my most personal affairs.
They were cold
the young knives
over whom
sits
sits
sits
mother England,
always seated
over millions of the wretched torn,
over poor tattered nations,
seated
over her ocean
reserved for private use,
sea of other people's
blood, toil, tears and sweat.
There seated in her old lace
sipping tea and listening to
the same old foolish tales
of princesses, coronations
and ducal unions.
Everything was a fairy tale.
Meanwhile death prowls in Victorian
hat and worn bones
through the black suburbs'

blackened maggot nests.
Meanwhile the police question you:
it's the word peace pierces them
like a bayonet.
That word peace
they wish to bury,
but for now they cannot.
They throw a shadow over it,
police fog,
they tie and cage it,
beat it,
splash it with blood and martyrdom,
interrogate it,
throw it into the deep sea
with a stone on each syllable,
burn it with an iron,
slash it with a saber,
throw at it vinegar, gall, lies,
box it up,
fill it with ash,
fling it off a cliff.
But then
the dove flies again:
peace with new plumage,
jasmine of the world
advancing with its petals,
the star of dream and labor,
the white bird
of purest flight,
rose that sails,
bread of all life,
star of all mankind.

2

The great love

Nevertheless,
England,
there is something of mahogany
in your waist,
old wood used
by the hand of man,
church pew, cathedral
choir in the fog.
Something
joins us to you,
there is something
contained
behind your windows,
a brusque wind,
a wild coastal bird,
a morning melancholy,
something impossibly lonely.
I loved the life
of your men, false
conquerors conquered,
poured to the four corners
of the planet
to fill your treasure chest.
Nevertheless,
if gold moved them
with its black wave
they were more than just that
but also people,

frail people in the darkness, alone,
while the royal standard's lions
smothered the peoples' battle.

Poor English children,
poor landlords
of a world threshed barren,
I know that the earthly nightingale
lives naturally
among you.
Shelley sings in the rain
and the rain adorns his scarlet lyre.
From your coast a dagger prow
points to the seas,
but on your shore the persecuted
found bread and built his house.
Lenin beneath the clouds
entering the Museum
seeking another line,
a date, a name,
while the whole world
seemed oppressed,
lonely solitude, impenetrable steppe,
there, with his eyeglasses
and his book,
Lenin,
changing fog into light.

And so you once were,
England,
tower of exile,
cathedral of refuge,
and those who now

use police
to close down lines and words,
hoarding wisdom's treasure –
those who deny your sand
to the wandering pilgrim of peace –
they are not worthy
of your ancient truth, of your wood.
They knife you,
killing all you shelter
within yourself,
not just your heart but your decency.

Homeland of sea birds,
you've taught me
all I know about birds.
You showed me
the fish's burnished scale,
the plenary treasure
of Nature,
you catalogued rivers, flowers,
mollusks and volcanoes.
To the fierce
regions of my homeland
came young Darwin,
with his lamp
his light illumined
beneath the earth
and the deep sea
all that we have:
plants, metals, lives
that weave the structure
of our dark star.
Later Hudson

in the meadows
busied himself with birds
forgotten by books
and little by little
filled the landscape
that gives us birth
with them,
England,
sweet explorer
of feathers and roots,
you became
passionate knowledge,
so now
why shelter
beneath your eaves
those birds of prey,
grave diggers,
destroyers of birds?
You ferreted out
the most secret
labyrinth
of life and lives,
and now,
when we hear
your voice
we hear ash,
dust, destruction, agony.
I know that you sing
and are
honest, plain like your lost folk
of suburbs and mines,
weighty and crackling
like the coal you dig up.

I beg you,
England,
be truly English
again,
do you hear me?
Yes, be England –
not Chicago,
not the police –
breathe,
be
what you have been
in your fields and villages,
a fruit orchard of birds and people,
plain folk,
refuge of the persecuted,
explorer of birds.

England,
I beg you
be a queen of the isles,
not an island vassal,
obey
your choir of maritime birds,
straightforward stock
of miners and sailors.
I will tell you in secret
that we wish to love you.
It is hard,
you know –
so many things happened
in the distant lands,
blood, exploitations,
and so on and so on.
And well, now,

in the hour of love
we wish to love you.
Prepare yourself as before
for the love that returns,
the love that rises within
the highest wave
of the human sea.
Prepare yourself
for peace,
and then,
be once again that which we love,
people like us,
a land like ours,
that's what we wish for.
We all
live
upon the earth
beneath the same forests,
upon the same sand.
We cannot
fight against autumn,
or battle
spring,
we have
to live
upon the same waves.

They are ours, mankind's,
the children's.
The waves
have no owner's seal,
nor does the land.
Therefore

in this fertile epoch,
time of destiny, invention,
let people of all races and regions
discover
great love
emblazon it
on land and sea.

XIV

BURNT LIGHT

1

The black flame

Today's rose is in
yesterday's promise on the branch.
It is clarity alone, structured light,
rushing brook of beauty,
small red ray
lifted above the soil.
Pines in the wind
spill their sound and needles,
sea salt gathers
the sky's overwhelming blue weight.

This day is peace,
broad and open and clear

like a new school building.
The wind is made of peace
crossing the pine tops.
Peace, my love, is the
light of your long hair
falling through my hands
when you lean your head and close,
for just a minute,
the doors of land,
sea and pines.
It's not a petal, not a rose,
not a black flash:
it's blood, now,
in this day far beyond the wind.

2

The storm-filled land

My love, my love, now
the thicket is pierced by
your eyes.
It is in Vietnam, a bitter
smell of burnt light,
a wind of perfume and burial.
Come forward
with your eyes,
open between lianas and sugar cane
the road of your eyes' ray.
I see
the tattered

heroes,
from sun to sun, without night,
without dew,
tiny captains
of sweat and gunpowder
defending the tangled skin,
the storm-filled land,
the country's flowers.

Vietnamese youth hidden
by the jungle, by silence
and by lies:
I don't deserve the sea,
I don't deserve
this day of peace and jasmine.
It is for you, for you,
the earthly treasure,
for all those
who took back their fatherland
inch by inch
from the invader and his fire
with their blood and their bones.
For them
the peace of the day and of the morning
joined in a corner of jungle or town
we shall have won for all mankind.

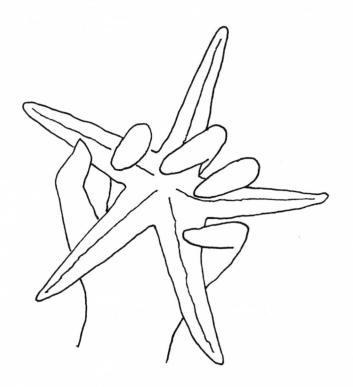

XV

THE SEA LAMP

1

A sky-colored port

When you disembark
in Lisbon,
sky-blue and rose-colored rose,
white and gold stucco,
brick petals,
the houses,
the doors,
the roofs,
the windows
splashed with lemon-tree gold,
overseas blue of the fleet.
When you disembark
you don't understand,

you don't know that
behind the windows
the mourning jailers
listen and
prowl,
rigid, going by the book,
herding prisoners to the islands,
condemned to silence,
swarming like shade squadrons
beneath green windows,
between blue hills,
the police beneath
the autumn horns of plenty
seeking Portuguese men,
scraping the ground,
dispatching men to darkness.

2

The forgotten zither

Oh lovely Portugal,
basket of fruit and flowers,
you surface
at the shore plaited by the ocean,
in the foam of Europe,
with the golden zither
that Camões left for you,
singing with sweetness,
scattering on Atlantic mouths
your wild vineyard scent,

seaside orange blossoms,
your shining moon broken up
by clouds and storms.

3

Prisons

But,
Portuguese man in the street,
just between us,
(no one can hear us) –
do you know where Álvaro Cunhal is?
Do you mark the absence
of the brave
Militao?
Portuguese girl,
you pass by
as if dancing
through the rose-colored
streets of Lisbon,
but –
do you know where Bento Gonçalves fell,
the purest of all Portuguese,
the honor of your sea and sand?
Do you know
that there is
an island,
Salt Island,
and Tarrafal turns

to darkness there?
Yes, you know it, young woman,
young man, yes, you know.
In silence
the word
walks slowly but covers
not only Portugal, but the whole Earth.
Yes we know,
in remote countries,
that for the past thirty years
a thick slab
like a tombstone or the tunic
of a bat-like cleric
has choked, Portugal, your sad song,
splashed your sweetness
with martyrs' drops
and covered your domes with shadow.

4

The sea and the jasmine

From your tiny hand
in other times
creatures emerged
released
into the wonder of the land.
So Camões returned
to leave for you a jasmine branch
that flourished yet.
Brilliance burned like your race's vineyard

of transparent grapes.
Guerra Junqueiro among the waves
let fall the thunder
of a wild freedom
bearing the ocean in his song,
and others multiplied
your rose-clustered splendor
as if from your narrow land
should come great hands
sowing seeds
throughout the world.

Even so,
time has buried you.
Clerical dust
layered in Coimbra
fell upon your orange ocean face
and covered the splendor
of your waist.

5

Maritime lamp

Portugal,
return to the sea, to your ships,
Portugal, return to mankind,
to the sailor, return to your land,
to your fragrance,
to your free thought in the wind,

again
at the morning light
of carnation and foam.
Show us your treasure,
your men, your women.
Hide no more the face
of your brave vessel
fixed firmly at Ocean's advance.
Portugal, navigator,
island explorer,
pepper cultivator,
discover the new man,
islands awakened,
discover the archipelago of time.
The sudden
appearance
of bread
on the table,
daylight, discover it,
you, explorer of the dawn.

How is this?

How can you deny
the sky your light, you that lit
the way of the blind?

You, sweet and iron-harsh and old,
narrow yet wide father of the horizon,
how can you close the door
to the new grape clusters
and the wind with stars from the East?

Europe's prow, seek
in the current
ancestral waves,
the sea-beard
of Camões.

Break
the spider's webs
that cover your fragrant rigging,
and then
for us children of your children,
those for whom
you discovered the dazzling geography
darkened until then,
show that you can cross anew
the dark sea
and discover mankind born
in the grandest islands of the world.
Sail, Portugal, the hour
has come, lift
your prow's stature
and become again
a path
between islands and men.
In this age gather
your light, become a lamp again:

And so you will learn once more to be a star.

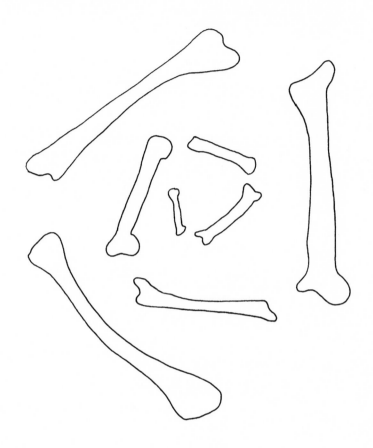

XVI

LAND, PAINTING

1

Arrival at Picasso's door

I came to Picasso at six in the morning,
an autumn day,
the sky announcing its rose opening,
and looking around I saw him
stretched out and burning
like dawn's fire.
Far behind
lay the blue mountain ranges
and between them lifting himself up
the ashen Harlequin valley.
Behold: I came from Antofagasta
and from Maracaibo,
I came from Tucumán
and from lower Patagonia,

icy teeth gnawed by the thunder,
that banner submerged
in perpetual snow.

And then I disembarked,
and I saw great apple-colored women
on Picasso's shores, boundless eyes,
arms I recognized:
perhaps the Amazonian,
perhaps the Form.

And to the West helpless puppets
rolling down toward yellow,
musicians all in musical frames,
and even more,
there dwelled beyond a heart-piercing
migration of women, artists,
petals and flames,
and in the midst of Picasso
between the prairies
and the glass tree,
I saw Guernica stained forever
with blood like a great river,
whose current swept to a horse's brow and a lamp:

burning blood climbs to the muzzles,
dampened light accusing forever.

So, then, in Picasso's lands
from South to West,
all life and lives came to a halt
and there the sea and the world
piled up grain and bloodshed.

I saw there the scratched chalk fragment,
the copper shell,
a dead horseshoe that grows
from its wounds to a metal eternity,
and I saw the soil enter like bread in the ovens
emerging with a sacred child.

I also found the black cockerel of encephalic foam,
with a branch of wire and slums,

the blue cat with its toenail fan,
the tiger creeping above the skeletons.

I recognized the quaking marks
of the river's mouth where I was born.
First the stone with thorns, where
it overflowed, illusory,
the loosened branch,
and the wood of broken ancestry
in which were born
the brusque birds of my natal fire.

But the bull poked out
from among the corridors in the earthly ring,
I saw its voice, it came prying into Picasso's worlds,
its effigy covered with shawls of violet ink,
and I saw coming the collar of its dark disaster
and all the embroidery of its unconquerable slime.

Picasso of Altamira, Orinoco Bull,
tower of waters hardened by love,
land of mineral hands turned as the plow,
moss innocence being born.

Here is the bull whose tail drags
the salt and gall,
and in its bullring
Spain's
collar shakes with a dry sound,
like a sack of bones
that the moon pours out.

Oh circle where silk still burns
like forgotten poppies in the sand
and there is nothing to confront
but day, time, land, destiny,
bull of the runaway air.
This bullfight is all purple mourning,
the wine banner that burst the vessels:
and yet more:
it is the dusty footstep of the mule driver
and the piled-up garments guarding
the distant silence of the charnel house.
Spain climbs on these stairways,
wrinkled gold and hunger,
the closed face of anger,
and yet more, examine their cape:
there are no eyelids.
But there is a black light, seeing us
yet without eyes.

Paloma's father, who came to the day
with her splayed out in the light,
newly lined upon her rose paper,
newly cleansed from blood and dew,
to the bright union of her banners.

Peace or dove, radiant appearance!

Circle, earthly union!

Pure sheaf among the red arrows!
Sudden direction of hope!
We are with you in the beaten depths
of clay, and today in the lasting
metal of hope.
"It is Picasso,"
says the fisherman, tying silver,
and the new autumn scrapes
the shepherd's standard:
the lamb that receives a leaf
from the Vallauris sky,
and hears the tradesmen
pass by their hive,
at once near the sea
and its cedar crown.

Our means are strong
when we toss – loving common man –
your hot coal onto the scales,
into the banner.
You face wasn't in the scorpion's plans.
It wished to strike at times
and met up with your boundless
crystal, your earthly lamp
and then?
Then by the shore of the land we grow,
toward the opposite ends of the Earth
we grow.

Whoever does not hear these steps hears yours.
Listen from time's infinitude to this path.
The land is wide.
Your hand is not alone.
The light is broad.
Light it above us.

2

To Guttuso, from Italy

Guttuso, the color blue came to your country
to learn what the heavens are and to understand
water.
Guttuso, light came from your country
and fire was born throughout the Earth.
In your country, Guttuso,
the moon has the scent of white grapes, honey,
fallen lemons,
but there is no land,
but there is no bread!

In your paintings you give
the land, the bread.
Good baker, give me your hand that lifts
the rose of flour above our banners.
Farmer, you have painted the land that you share.
Fisherman, your throbbing harvest moves
from your brushes toward the homes of the poor.
Miner, you have drilled darkness with an iron
flower,

and you return with spattered face
to give us the hardness of the hollowed out
nighttime.
Soldier, wheat, and gunpowder upon the cloth,
you defend the way.

In your paintings the peasants of the South
march toward the land!
People without a land, toward the earthly star!
Men without faces who in your paintings have a
name!
Eyelids of battle who advance toward the fire!
Bread of the fight, fists of anger!
Hearts of the land crowned
by the electricity of new sheaves!
Grave step of the people toward the morrow,
toward decision, toward becoming men,
to sow, to milk, leaving in your painting their first
portrait.

These – "What are their names?"
From the old walls of your country
the great-necked men of wicked sword ask,
"Who are they?"
And from her rotunda sugar-breasted regal Paulina,
naked and cold –
"Who are they?" she asks.
"We are the land," say the furrows.
"Today we exist," says the reaper.
"We are the people," sings the day.

I ask you, "Are we alone?"
And the countenance you left

among other campesinos responds:
"Surely not!"
And it isn't true that you, solitary violin,
failed nocturne, seeing yourself in the ghostly
image,
wish to fly lest your feet hold fast to
fragments, earth, forests and battles!
Ay, with these shoes I have marched with you
measuring cemeteries and markets!

I knew a Nicaraguan painter.
The trees there are stormy
and shed their blooms like green volcanoes.
The rivers crush
in their current rivers over-laden
with butterflies, and the jail cells
are filled with screams and wounds!
And this painter came to Paris,
painted a dot of pale ochre
on canvas, white, white, white,
and on that a mark, a mark, a mark.
He came to see me then
and I became sad,
because behind that little man and his dot
Nicaragua was weeping,
with no one to hear,
Nicaragua buried her sorrows
and her slaughter in the jungle.

Paintings, paintings for our heroes, for our dead!
Paintings the color of apple and blood for our
people!
Paintings with the faces and hands
we know and wish not to forget!

And so let arise the color of our meetings,
the movement of our flags,
the victims of the police.
Let the workers' meetings
be praised and painted and inscribed,
the strike at noon, the fishermen's treasure,
the stoker's night, the strides of victory,
the tempest of China,
the unlimited breath of the Soviet Union,
and man:
each man with his task and his lamp,
in the safety of his land
and of his bread.

I embrace you, brother,
because in your realm you fulfill the destiny
of Italy's battle and light.
Let the morning wheat
paint with golden lines
the people's peace upon the land.
Then, when the air
stirs on a wave the harvest of the world
bread will sing on all the plains.

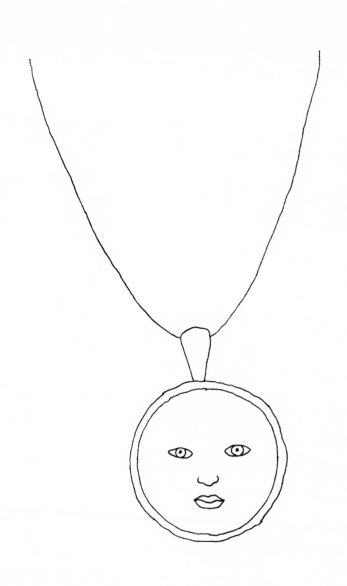

XVII

HONEY OF HUNGARY

1

I came from afar

I carried on my back
a sack
of black sufferings,
the night time of my country's
mines.
When coal
from Lota
burns
in a locomotive
it turns red
and the burning
isn't fire,
it's blood,

the blood of my country's miners,
black blood that accuses.
And so
doubled over with my black burden
laden with blood and coal I traversed
the streets of Europe,
the silver moon worn down
by human eyes,
the old bridges broken
by war, the empty cities
their windows holes
and their rubbish where grass grows,
nettles,
sad yellow hedges,
fearful,
without roots.
And so I went through the bombed-out streets
seeking green hope,
until I found it
dressed in water and gold
one day
by the double banks of Budapest.

2

The years grow

Hungary,
your face is doubled like a medallion.
I found you in the summer
and your visage

was
forest and wheat:
quick summer
with its mantle of gold
covered over your sweet green body.
Later
I saw you full of snow,
oh beauty blushing pink
with white teeth and white crown,
winter star,
land of whiteness!

And so I loved your face,
double medallion,
passing my kisses over your pupils,
welcome in the dawn,
because you were building
the sun as it rose,
your flag,
the stride of your people
on the steppes, pure tools
of liberation, the steel
of which stars are made.

This age grows
alongside me,
this epoch
like a quickening forest,
like a volcanic plant
filled with life and leaves,
my epoch
of blood and clarity, from cold night
and resplendent morn.

New cities grow,
banners awake,
the socialist republics
establish themselves as they march,
Vietnam throbs
because a new life is born
in blood and sorrow.

Laurel and moon
fill my era,
love and dust!

I have seen
rebirth,
growth,
the old lands bearing
robust new things.
I think
upon the lost man
of another era
who saw nothing born,
who threw himself from street to street,
from night to cold night,
climbed stairs,
filled himself with smoke,
and never saw where the steps
or smoke ended.
That man
was like a fungus in the jungle,
in the wet darkness
he wasted his heritage,
saw not the height above the forest
tattooed with stars,

nor saw below his feet
all the intertwined seedlings
of the forest.
I sense, I see, I touch
the growth of all that survives,
I travel from one land to another testifying,
summing up the ineffable,
adding the steps,
connecting the syllables
of the song of the wind upon the earth.

3

Forward!

USSR,
China,
people's Republics,
oh socialist
world,
my
world,
produce,
make trees, canals,
rice, steel,
grains, factories,
books, engines,
tractors and cattle.
Draw your fish from the sea
and from the rich land your harvests
more golden than the world.

Let your barns
shine forth
from the stars like mines discovered,
let feet pound on the planet
like a jackhammer's
rhythmic assault,
let coal leave its cradle
with a red shout
reaching to the great foundries,
and let bread overflow
each day,
let there be pure oceans
of honey and meat,
let the green wheels of the machines
fit ocean's axles.
Seek beneath the snow,
and in the height,
so that your wings of shining peace
might fill the farthest spheres
of the heavenly country
with motorized music
.I live in a world of hate.
I read the newspaper of hate.
They wish
that a sudden wind would
destroy your harvests.
That your cities not be rebuilt.
They want
your trucks to stall
so no bread or wine can come
to your villages' myriad mouths.
The want to deny you water,
life, air.
Therefore,

socialist man, awake,
awake smiling,
crowned with flowers and factories,
upright among all
the fruit of the world.

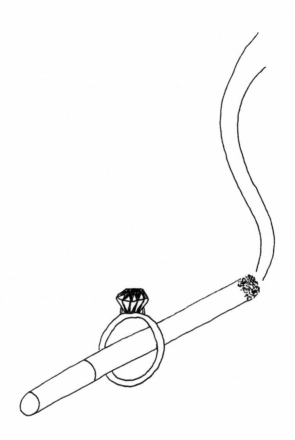

XVIII

FLOWERING FRANCE, RETURN!

France, jadis on te soulait nommer
En tous pays, le trésor de noblesse
Par un chacun pouvoit en toi trouver
Bonté, bonheur, loyauté, gentillesse,
Clergie, sens, courtoisie, proesse.
Tous etrangiers amoient te suir.
Et maintenant voy dont j'ay desplaisance...

CHARLES D'ORLÉANS (1430)

1

The season begins

When the seasons
are prepared
beneath the ground,
sap, roots,
seeds,
fire,
water
all speak
seeking finery,
polishing the future
mahogany and hazel,
hardening the snow-white marble
of the almond trees,
weaving the threads
of the nets,
lifting grape clusters'
green sugar,
then
all is ready:
red-handed autumn

or pure spring
or river summer
or star-colored winter,
France opens her doors:
time has begun.

For there are the loveliest
dances of leaves,
crackling silk of forest autumn.
There the waters
know to sing in harmony
with the violin and the wind.
Cathedral and plain
now for many years
flourished receiving
the same double kiss of rain.
Wine is born there
in the French countryside
and words find
ripe crystal form and sound
in limpid goblets
as the people sing.

There
the people sing always.

Then came war
like relentless pitch,
but France's grief
emerged in song.
The brave sang
against the firing wall.
The Communards sang.

Headless, Jean Richard's
daughter sang.
France's people sing,
while Atlantic merchants
make ready the slaughter.

But you are not simply
a room for spacious autumn
or bejeweled spring,
garden of France,
street of France,
fighter,
but have written your name
with stone and blood
on destiny's wall,
and as full streams
of harmony run sure in you,
so also your people,
in plenitude, from shore to shore,
overflowing with battles and gifts,
will restore joy, singing.

2

And nevertheless

In my life I've made use
of Rabelais
as I would tomatoes.
For me
his carnivorous trumpet

was critical,
his principal uproar.
And yet ...
Alone that night,
I passed by on the coast
of the wealthy poor,
in the crazed South of France.

I came earth-bound,
with the dust of the South, red snow,
orange blossom of all roads.
I was happy.
I awoke
with the golden collar
of joy
beneath my left arm,
with the purple stem of a rose
beneath my new kisses,
and then
the police,
being very proper,
offered me cigarettes
and threw me out of France.

That was after my first night
in France. Between her land
and my sleeping body
time had passed
and that night, in dreams,
the earth rose up to me
with verse and wine,
vine shoots and roots.

Ancient dead beloved,

saffron and jasmine,
enveloped me asleep,
and I sailed through Earth's scents,
crossing over,
until day with white shoulder
and drops of dew came
and then
who came?
No one other than her,
France today,
the police,
and even though the anchored ship
waited for me to return to Chile,
there, between cigarettes,
they deported me
and nearly all that I love,
and nothing helped me save
the memory
of Charles d'Orléans,
cleansing each day
his mournful guitar,
it didn't matter that
Rimbaud lived hidden
in my house,
for many years.
Oh but nothing,
nothing.
Not Éluard's eyes
like two beams of blue fire
above my shoulders.
Nothing helped.
The police
spoke of orders from on high,

that it was quite clear:
I could never return.
I could not
set one foot on that forbidden land.
I should understand this:
neither transit,
nor fly above,
nor cross below,
nor whisper by the sea,
to the Normandy waves I love.
I cannot
enjoy a tree or receive rain,
sleep by the watercress.
I cannot sing alongside a river
or cry from joy.
I cannot
eat fresh cheese
with lip-like lettuce. I cannot
drink white wine
on the Île Saint-Louis,
no, not
one more day
of my life.

They were entirely clear
and completely obscure.
They threw me out. That was clear.
But why? Obscure.
So, the police
took in their hands
the rosette of another age
that the Count of Dampierre
had placed in my lapel,
they looked on it

as if it were a filthy curse
or a cigarette butt tasting of ham.
They had
orders
from on high,
and so it was, ladies and gentlemen,
that I left France.
It's normal,
I needn't
explain myself.

We all know
that the Embassy of the Far West,
with its cowboys,
spits on the crystal chandeliers
in Versailles.
That with tobacco in his mouth
Jim Coca-Cola
pees on the statues
of Fontainebleau, the blind statues
of sleeping queens.
We all know that,
but,
I don't wish to speak of it,
it's not my theme.

If I were
twenty years old
and they had tossed me thus
by the waist
out of France,
this would be a long
lament, a lengthy dirge.

I would have written
death and funeral rites
of the most fragrant
spring.

But, now,
with so many scars
that have not yet managed
to kill my heart,
with joy
still unwoken between my arms,
with all life before me,
with hope,
with all that is yet to come
when we ourselves are no more,
with France who tomorrow
will also awake,
because she has never slept,
with all the jasmines and the vineyards,
the streets, the roads,
and the songs I love,
and that no one least of all
the police
can wrench from my soul,
I can say, ladies
and gentlemen,
that I love sweet France,
whence they expelled me.
And that I continue
living
as if I lived there,
with its land and its heroes,
with its wine and its people,
and that I have not officially awoken

from that single night
in which all the scent
of her depth and sweetness
rose up in my dream to bid me adieu.

3

More than one France

Limpid
is the land:
water bubble and iron,
green
ocean cup, plains,
distances,
waves
of quartz and copper
becalmed in her.
Coal in the depth
of blind tunnels
held its energy.
Fruits and grains
like the shawl
of an ancient queen
cover her with yellow stars:

the land's cup overflows:

they switch on
and switch off

all light and
all shadow,
bitter, with winter
thorns, sweet,
full of all
sweetness:
planet, you guard something
more alive
and electric
than all metals:

it is man,
the tiny
being who shivers,
falls and lifts
his wounded brow
and with arm newly scraped
grasps lightning bolts.
I see
the hot forests,
the jungle
in Laos,
insects like leaves,
leopards
of silent strength
and phosphoric waist,
great plaited trees
in the ancient soil,
moist monuments
with broken noses
and eyes
erupting branches.

None of that

interests us:
pay attention,
wait,
look!
Here is what you love:
One small
free man
with a rifle,
waiting.
It is he,
the Cambodian
guerilla.
He awaits
the armored invader's
mechanical step.
He doesn't think
about the stalking beast,
the serpent
with electric venom:
he only awaits
the foreign soldier.
There in the jungle
the leaves
are his country,
each sound of bird
or water,
each flicker
of butterfly or eyelid,
is his country.
His country is the foliage
and in its shade
the man,
the small man,

defending
each day
one of its leaves.
Vietnam is on the other side.
There are gray-brown rivers,
fluttering with life and messages
going from land to land.
The French
in the cities
hear the leaves' whisper.
Why did they leave
the fruit spring of France?
They told them
they must bring
their culture
and thereafter
Eisenhower's
machine guns
and napalm,
ruin and flame,
disembarked with them,
the French.
Victor Hugo's
nephews
brought not
books
but
horrid bullets,
sorrows,
blood.

Therefore
a black murmur
of smoke and fear

arises from Saigon
crosses the land
and falls
on France,
the fear of Indochina
falls on some small
poor homes.

Death,
an obituary notice,
comes
like a black eagle
from Asia's heights
and enters
the French spring morning
with a rapid claw
shadow.

4

Henri Martin

Henri Martin hears
the rumor
of fear and blood.

In his French prison
he hears
the forest banners.
His people die
uselessly,
they rot, tin-colored beetles

carry them away.
Far away
fall
the sons of France.
Why?
Henri Martin opposed
the honorless
slaughter,
and now in striped suit,
with a number on his shoulders,
the radiant
honor of France
labors imprisoned.

To unload in a hot
downpour,
among the mosquitos,
tanks and pustules,
curses, woes,
to unload
boys
born of the rose
of France,
sons
of jasmine and grapes,
to kill them,
to decorate them
and assassinate them,
the little government
of France
must crucify honor,
imprison it,
clothe it in prison garb,
number it,

industrialize its dunghill
to sell it
to the Washington cowboys,
break the bones
of ancient
honor never before extinguished.
Therefore
Henri Martin,
radiant,
indomitable
through the bars
that imprison
the tricolor eyes
of his people,
sees
how blood falls
in the swamps,
far away,
without glory,
beneath torrid wings,
and the beetles
with their tiny
tin mouths
ferrying
to their moist dens,
men,
parts of boys,
the strength and sweetness
of France
sacrificed
so Philadelphia cowboys
can dance with the French ambassador's
sultry wife.

Henri Martin: the clover
of morning grass,
the humblest things,
the carpenter's
bench,
the nameless blue flower
between the stones,
the terrible
sulfur wind
from Chuquicamata in the night,
men
heaped up
in the mines,
bread,
the guerillas
of our sorrowful,
maternal, wretched,
heroic
Greece today,

all

that is simple,
that which sings in all lands and rivers
without the need to learn or know,

all

salute you,
Henri Martin, brother
of whatever exists, brother
of clarity and dream,
brother

of what is right and of the day,
brother of all hope,
sailor.

I pass by and see the world,
There I was,
there where you were.
I know
blood and death.
Therefore, because you are
my brother for life,
Henri Martin, France's
honor, leaf
of the highest oak,
laurel of the plains,
hero
of peace and purity,
I salute you
in the simplicity
of the sand and snow
of my distant home.

XIX

NOW SINGS THE DANUBE

... Danubio, río divino
que por fieras naciones
vas con tus claras ondas discurriendo.

GARCILASO DE LA VEGA, Canción III

1

Burnt fingers

Ancient Romania, golden Bucharest,
how you resemble
our infernal and celestial
republics
in America!

You were pastoral and somber.
Thorns and roughness shielded
your terrible misery,
while Mme. Charmante
rambled through the French salons.
The whip fell
on the scars of your people,
while the refined writers
of their journal *Sur* safely
studied Lawrence, the spy,
or Heidegger or "notre petit Drieu."
"Tout allait bien à Bucarest."

Oil
left burns on your fingers
and blackened the faces
of nameless Romanians,
but it made a sterling silver choir
in New York and London.
Thus
was Bucharest so elegant,
its women so suave.
"Ah quel charme, monsieur."
Meanwhile hunger
prowled about lifting
its empty fork in the black outskirts
and the wretched countryside.
There, sí señores, it was
just like Buenos Aires,
like Santiago or Lima,
Bogotá and São Paulo.
A few of them danced in the hall
exchanging sighs,
the Club and the literary journals
were very European,
the hunger was very Romanian,
the cold was Romanian,
the suffering of the poor
in the common grave was Romanian,
and so its life went on
from flower to flower
as in my continent with prisons filled
and waltzes in the gardens.

Oui, Madame, what a world
it was, what irreparable
loss to all the important people!

Bucharest is no more.
That gusto, that lineage,
that exquisite mix
of rottenness and *patisserie*!
Terrible, it seems to me.
They tell me that
even the local color,
the picturesque ragged costumes,
the twisted beggars
like wretched roots,
little girls shivering
waiting at night
at the doors of the dance hall,
all that, what a horror,
has disappeared.

What shall we do, *chère Madame*?
Sometime let's do
an issue of *Sur* about how cattlemen are
deeply worried about *métaphysique*.

2

The mouth that sings

I come from the pine groves
to the Danube's low mouth,
blue air shaking
lives and life.
The air cleanses the salons' depth,

a breeze
from the people's banners
enters the windows.
Erasing with your hands,
in that moment,
Romania, the rags
of your people, you have shown
a new head, new eyes,
new mouth that sings,
and you show in the land today
not only a shepherd's race,
but a shining army marching forth.

3

A printing house

I saw a printing house arise
as powerfully
as would a bank in my country.
I saw it take on the form
of that cathedral brick by brick
from the word,
raise up its walls
and soon
let shine its linotype machines,
the well-oiled steel,
the press itself rolling as
a grand typographic tank.

It was lovely
to see the entrance
of this iron mother
of written light.
Grinding
she advanced
and at her side,
like blue ants,
the workers.
She had the scent
of wind
with iron oil,
new fruit
and silence,
the scent of a great time to come.
She was lovely,
more beautiful than the leaves
and the trees,
more beautiful than the flowers,
see how the press marches
toward the height.
There where the grand dames
bowed as in old times
before a small wastrel of Europe,
King Carol,
there a printing house
grew like
a wind cathedral
grander
than a Bank of the West,
grander than a rifle
factory,
more beautiful
than a greenhouse of fiery lilies,

higher
than our American trees.

4

The river gods

Let Ovid and Garcilaso exiled
yesterday upon your shores
crown you, Romania,
crown you and sing.
Let your river carry the waters
nourishing lives and sand,
love peopling your homes and your forests,
with grape clusters
covering your arms and your breast.

I celebrate not only the free people
of your new cities and farmlands,
I dedicate my song
not only to the creative works
of schools and factories,
I consecrate my lyric
not only to the canals
opened in the rock and the soil
that the waters of the Danube
may spread new growth –
but to you, Romania,
to your noble taste of earth and wine,
to your bread sown liberally
among your people,

the smell of pines and mimosas
that the wind gifts you.
I sing
to the skin of your grapes,
the brightness of the eyes
that join with mine
like two black rays,
your ancient dances
shining today in the light you conquered
like flowers or fire,
to the friendship of all,
to the serene hand of the Party,
to the joy
of Romanian peace,
to your endless memory
that sings like a river.

Romania,
today I write you this letter
from the sands of my country.
Receive it, Romania.
It carries the splash of the Pacific,
carries voices and kisses,
carries snow from the highest mountains,
carries songs and struggles
of my people.

Honor and love, Romania,
arise in you like two new vines.

Knowledge shines in your eyes.
In your mouth grape clusters smile.

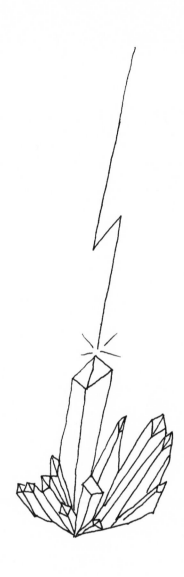

XX

THE ANGEL OF THE CENTRAL COMMITTEE

1

Guardian angel

In my house, as a little boy they told me:
"Listen. There is an angel who goes with you
and defends you:
your Guardian Angel."

I grew up, grieving, in the corners.
And the piled-up dirge fell
drop by drop in my writings.
As a teen I went from danger to danger,
from night to night,
with my own sword defending my bread
and my poem,
cutting around the place in the dark street
I needed to cross,
amassing my solitary strength in the emptiness.

Who came to my door
but to break something?
Who didn't bring me acid lava?
Who didn't carry poisonous stones
at the speed of my existence?

The owner tossed me out in wrath.
The elegant disdained my face.
And from their little Mexican copybooks,
or from ash-grey notebooks,
bearded and malicious, merchants
of dead roses, poets
without poetry, they let slip ink
against my fighter's hair.
They opened wells of a miry soul
so that I'd fall between their teeth,
they crowned my song with knives,
but I didn't wish to flee,
or defend myself:
I sang, I sang filling myself with stars,
I sang with no one to defend me,
save the blue steel of my song.

2

Then you hid yourself

Where are you, my Guardian Angel?
Were you the thorn home I was supposed to sleep in?
Were you the table of poverty they prepared for me?
Were you the hatred, unending wire I had to cut,

or perhaps you were the misery of wretched folk,
that I kept finding along the roads, in the cities,
in the trenches of the abandoned?
Ay, you were invisible, since only in the blows of
hardship,
only smashing inhuman portals,
did I see the voice of all voices grow within me,
and I went out among the living to the battle.

3

I left my country

I crossed the cordillera on horseback.

A petty tyrant, a fast dancer sold
my homeland
metal and minerals and all
and filled with walls and prisons
dawn's domain.
I left through throats clawed
by nature, galloping
beneath the silence of a dark grove,
dovecotes hurled of a sudden
out of snowdrifts, frozen feathers,
a purity of power:
and quickly land and trees
became harsh foes and scars,
quickly turned into wooden cutwaters,
impenetrable thickness
woven like a cathedral

between the leaves,
or a colossus of slippery salt,
or a toothless belt of stone.

Yet more, I descended quickly
the steep-sloping land,
and the horsemen
with their axes opened the road,
where the vertiginous god of a new river
overflowing with swords waited,
launching its hidden music
over the thicket.

4

First appearance of the angel

And there crossing the river,
when the waters bent
the horses' gallops,
suddenly a gust of wind struck
like an arrow in my throat,
the animal stumbled
and the waters at my side
were like a torrent of needles,
the waterfall waiting like
a lightning bolt on the rocks,
there I looked behind me,
and saw for the first time the angel,
unshaven, wrinkled,
with a pistol and a lasso.
The angel guarded me,

he walked wingless beside me,
the angel of the Central Committee.

5

The solitary angel

He defended himself
against the indomitable air,
against the river,
against the hurricane-wind stones
and the thorn-rough lands.
He defended me, the angel,
against the hounds that hated me,
who waited howling for
my blood in the criminal streets.

6

Angel of the plains

Oh unapproachable moon,
on the prairies,
oh blue sun above all space,
plain of solitude,
straight-line star
stretched on a desert immensity.

Argentine grass, endless plain,
the smell of cereal sky,
road made of all roads,
wide lidless spring.

I went from end to end,
trembling in my swiftness,
crossing the planet's day
and naked night.

And there lost in the distance,
when the wandering ostrich
or wild-land dove appeared,
when weariness and solitude filled
the plain's clear cup,
when I felt helpless at the end,
when I was but absence,
dream, sweat and dust,
going on toward freedom with open eyes,
with another face,
hands tied to the wheel,
without sleep yet smiling
through the night,
there he was again,
there guarding against my fatigue:
I don't know his name,
perhaps López,
perhaps Ibieta,
the angel of the Central Committee.

7

Angel of the rivers

Perhaps you know that I passed
along America's iron rivers.
The unfolding Paraná
received me trembling.
Its slowness was like the moon
when it spills beyond the plains
and it was peopled with secret lips
that kissed its wild movements.

Territorial rivers,
red sons of America's
moist darkness,
I came to your waters,
to the blood that night and day
carries your multiple names
to fight the sands,
I came an Equatorial branch,
a piece of your land,
river foliage.

The wide waters told me
their Paraguayan blood song
and from Asunción the towers
spoke martyrdom:
just as a bog changes a thicket,
as petroleum stains the flag
and as oil and mud flow
over the dead poor of the country.

And the river told me
what the dead say
speaking from the roots,
begging for help though dead,
holding buried banners
while foreigners with their petroleum
drink in the palace
with the executioner.

There among the rivers I found you,
the rivers ran even inside my own blood
reckoning the pages of the forest,
and there, new angel,
you were in the depth of America.
Not recognizing you,
"Comrade angel, is it you?" I said,
and through great lands,
wheat, threats, waves and pines
we passed together
until I too closed my eyes
upon the sea and flew sleeping.

8

Poetry angel

Soviet Union,
you flourish with other flowers
that as yet have no earthly name.

Your strength
the flower of a steel tree.

Your brotherhood
the flower of fragrant bread.
Your winter
a flower in which the snow brings
light to love without fear.
I covered the land where Pushkin
lifted crystal light anew in song,
and I saw how his people
lifted that constellation above hands
used to lifting wheat.

Pushkin,
you were the angel of the Central Committee.
With you I visited holy ruins
where your people's soldiers
defended the syllables of your soul.

With you I saw grow from rubbish
the giant flight of life,
the tractor wheels toward autumn,
new cities filled with sounds,
yellow planes like bees.

And when I entered a museum or a home,
or a factory,
or the river that singing follows you,
or when in Lenin's city I saw erased
the scars of stately martyrdom,
oh guileless comrade,
you were by my heart giving me all
the proud stature of your country.

There, in the end,
an angel carried no more of a weapon
than a crystal lightning branch
and he and all his land defended
the wandering syllables of my song.

There at last peace protected me.

And Pushkin said to me:
"Come with me to Novosibirsk,
there in the desert lands,
peopled before by solitude and pain,
today the banner of my voice passes
over the proud towers."

Angel, you wished me to visit the whole land,
touching the young sheaves,
counting factories and schools,
conversing with children and soldiers.

9

Angel Vyka

Hirsute angel of Poland, Vyka,
I must ask you these questions:
crossing through the whole life of your country,
the burning splendor of iron ruling in Katowicz,
the wheat fields stretching in waving joy
above the whole land,
the processions of medieval Catholicism,
the smoke of the coal region, the air in Krakow,
dry free air, the Baltic once again
pressing its white wings and waves
between new cranes,
the brick mixed with the dust
of infinite destruction
lifting again to the sky over Warsaw,
and the metallic smell of the pines
above the Masurian Lakes,
plain witnesses of the slaughter,
and from village to village
on ruined architecture mankind
restored the beauty of your land,
filling the silence with the seeds of your rebirth.
This fertility unhoped for until yesterday,
this milk given from mouth to mouth like a new
sign,
and that land that sings and is shared
without escaping like water,
but granting metals and grains,
tell me, angel Vyka,

you who accompanied my steps
with careless heart,
what do you have, what must we hide,
why do they wish to deny these regions,
these harvests, this simple honey,
why do they wish to erase grandeur
and reject this human victory?
Each day you were the silent angel
friend of the hidden race,
just so that the forest might protect
the smallest tips of your strawberries
for your companion of other seas,
or that the round shell might enter
my naturalist's sensibilities,
and so you showed me all your open land
lit up like a smile
among the sands and pine groves,
by the seaside of Gdansk,
among the trucks.

10

Oh comrade angel

Solitary warrior, angel of all
latitudes, you appear
each time in the mine's grave hollows,
when oppression and fatigue
bend your arms,
and you lift your mineral
wings like a shield.

In that shadow between the villages
your charted flight
crosses the harsh thorn lands,
the black barbed wire of death.
Comrade, the one who is failing awaits you,
the one who guards his strength awaits you,
the one who escapes danger
and the one who returns to it.
You are in the midst of a tempest time,
of anger with a worn hat,
in all the world,
with your wings ready beneath the common
light of a poor jacket.
You are the sum of these fates.

Over all the land you fly.

No one recognizes you
save those who also read
dawn's radiant scripture
in the black night.
Without seeing you many men pass by you,
by the corner where leaning against a wall
you are the road or a nameless tree
in the human forest.

But they who come to you
know you exist.
And they, behind shared eyes,
perceive the people's sword.

And so in full light
you receive us all
in the free regions of the East,
not like exiles,
but smiling to give us
peace, bread,
the keys of the kingdom.

XXI

A MEMORIAL OF THESE YEARS

1

Paul's death came

I've just learned
of Paul Éluard's death.
Here, in a telegram's
tiny envelope.
I closed my eyes, it was
his death, some letters,
and a great white void.

Death is just so,
his death's arrow
air-winged passing
through my fingers,
wounding me like the thorn
of a terrible rose.

Hero or bread, I don't recall
whether his crazed sweetness
was that of the crowned victor
or simply honey that is shared.
I do recall his eyes,
drops from that cerulean ocean,
flowers of a blue cherry tree,
ancient spring.

How many things pass through land
and time to make a man.
Rain, shore birds whose hoarse cry
resounds in the foam,
towers,
gardens and battles.

That
was Éluard: a man
to whom the rays of rain had come,
vertical threads of the elements,
and a mirror of classical water
in which reflected and flowered
the tower of peace and beauty.

2

Now we know

All day we know, all night,
all month we know, all year we know.

In another age man
was isolated,
pleasure covered his ears,
Heaven claimed him,
Hell called to him,
and besides all that
the human landscape
was dark.
He couldn't say for certain
whether the others
were men,
men of the islands,
those far away,
those who of a sudden displayed
on an elephant's tusk as much wisdom
as the door of a cathedral.

But
there far
between clouds and smoke,
the colonies,
the plants themselves,
mixed
with reptile skins.

Now
it's all different.
Poor friend,
you know,
you know that mankind exists.
Each day
they ask you for a signature
to pluck a living soul

from a living prison,
and overwhelmed
you come to know
the underground tunnels
of the land.
You know, we know,
each day we know,
we understand even when asleep:
it is now impossible
to cover our ears
with Heaven.
The land visits us
in the morning
and gives us breakfast:
blood and dawn,
darkness or building,
war or farming,
and one must choose, my friend,
each day,
knowing now,
knowing full well now
where both new life
and old death
may be found.

3

Here comes Nazim Hikmet

Nazim, newly freed
from prison, he gave me his shirt,

embroidered with gold threads,
red like his poetry.

Threads of Turkish blood
are his verses,
true fables
with ancient inflection,
curved or straight,
scimitars or swords,
his secret verses
made to confront
with all the light of midday,
today like secret weapons,
they shine beneath the floors,
they wait in the wells,
beneath the impenetrable darkness
of the dark eyes of his people.
He came from his prison
to become my brother
and together we compassed
the stepped snows
and burning night with our own lamps.

Here is his portrait that his
form not be forgotten.

It is high
like a tower
lifted in peace from the plains
and high up
two windows:
his eyes
with Turkey's light.

Wanderers
we found
the earth firm beneath our feet,
the land conquered
by heroes and poets,
the streets of Moscow,
the full moon flowering on the walls,
the girls
we loved,
the love we adored,
joy,
our own sect,
the complete hope we shared,
and more than all
the fight
of people
everywhere one drop and another drop,
drops from the sea of mankind,
his verses and my verses.

But
behind Nazim's joy
are deeds,
deeds like timbers
or building foundations.
Years
of silence and prison.
Years
unable
to chew, to eat, to drink
his heroic youth.

He told me
that for more than ten years

they left him
in the light of a bare electric bulb
all night and day
forgotten each night,
left alone
but with the light burning.
His joy has black roots
sunk deep in his country
like a flower in the swamp.
Therefore when he laughs,
when Nazim laughs,
Nazim Hikmet,
it is not as when you laugh:
his laugh is whiter,
the moon laughs in him,
a star, wine,
the deathless soil,
all rice hails his laughter,
all the people sing through his mouth.

4

Albania

I was never
in Albania,
harsh beloved country,
stony
shepherd's land.
Today

I hope
to come to you as to a feast day,
a new
earthly feast day: the sun
over the muscular hilt
of your mountain ranges,
and to see among the boulders
how the soft young lily grows,
culture,
letters stretched out,
respect for the ancient peasant,
the worker's cradle,
the illustrious monument
of brotherhood, the growth
of goodwill like a young plant
that flowers in impoverished old lands.

Albania, small,
strong, firm and sonorous,
your string on the guitar
-- thread of water and steel –
unites the sound of your history,
to the song of invincible time,
with a voice of forests
and buildings,
aromas and whiteness,
song of the whole man
and the whole forest,
birds and apple trees,
winds and waves.

Strength, firmness and flower
are your gift in the building of the world.

5

India 1951

In India
again,
another time
the smell
of dead fruit,
crows
cawing.
I sensed
my heart
pressed within me
as in a broken glass,
I heard footsteps,
steps that have died,
footsteps.
A thicket
of races and tunics,
India,
maternal, enmeshed,
solemn, cruel, remote,
you are the same.
The great rivers burying bodies,
saffron color in the hills,
but now
was not my youth, my lonely
wandering adolescence.
Now
flowers awaited me,
they fell upon my neck,

and a name,
a letter,
a simple syllable
came
from the prison cell to recognize me.

Lands of Telenghana,
martyrs, creatures
caught between
two fires,
the government's machine guns,
the prisons
of Nizam and Hyderabad.
Peasants fallen
in lands they thought
their own,
now
with their own Parliament,
without the English,
and the old misery,
the hunger
howling in the villages.
Waiting,
India has
always lived
waiting,
seated by
the river of time,
waiting.

The fighters passed
on bloodied feet,
the pearl-eating
princes,

the impassive English,
the cold priests
like reptiles,
studying the navel
of earth and sky,
all
devouring something,
passengers, pirates, mercenaries,
and you, mother of the world,
seated by the river
of time,
weaving and waiting.

Now
the poets,
Sirdard Jaffris or the other,
thin or bearded,
were leaving their cells.
Poetry
in India
entered the dungeon,
left and returned,
teaching
freedom among the prisoners,
knowing
the sufferings,
the dialects, the sorrows,
the secret words
of self-absorbed peasants,
woeful groans,
open wounds,
rebellious gentleness
advancing to lift its standard
of stars and doves.

Womb of the world, closed
region where history's
grapes ferment.
Ancient sister
of the old planets,
I found out now,
listening to the songs in the villages,
the scattered wraths,
the fists in the wind,
I found that
your heights will rise,
your power will gather,
you will give to your people
the bread you denied them,
and no more shall we see
hunger crossing behind your gold,
the shining rite
of the gods' theogony,
hunger with its broom
sweeping poor bones and garbage
to the side of the road.

India, lift
your youth,
set your watch to mark the coming hour.
Go forward and seize
the hour of high noonday.

Your arrows are ancient.

Lift them to your brow
and fix your destiny on time's clock.

6

Dawn from Dobris

In Dobris, near to Prague,
speaking with
Jorge Amado,
my companion of years and battles:
"Where are you
coming from now?"

I, from the wide rivers
of Guatemala and Mexico,
from the green brightness
of the River Dulce, within.
He carried
the fire of wild birds,
dew
from its delta.

I recounted my travels.
He was returning
from Bulgaria, bringing
the light of red rose bushes
in his breast,
and he told stories,
of men, business,
socialism on the march
in that
bristly land, now building.

It was late, the hot coals

burned in the stone hut.
Outside
the wind stirred whispering
the leaves on the beech trees.

Persecuted,
we pilgrimaged together,
and behold peace
has brought us back together.

We had bread,
light,
fire,
soil,
a castle.
They weren't ours alone,
they belonged to all.

We didn't want
to speak. The wind spoke for us.
It stretched itself
throughout the forest,
flying
with detached leaves.

The wind
taught,
singing
what we were,
what we were and what we had.

Terrestrial clarity
surrounded us.

Solemn was the silence.

The paths had been long.

And so the dawn beat
upon the windows anew
to go with us
throughout the world.

Epilogue

The song shared

Between the cordillera
and the deep Chilean sea
I write.

The white mountain range.
Sea the color of iron.

I returned from my journeys
with new grapes.

And the wind.

The wind shook
the land, the roots.

I traveled with the wind.

Today between sea and snow
and my land
I shared the gifts
I found in the world.

I settled my love
over my homeland's
spring like a burning bramble.

I returned singing.

Where I was, creative
life
clothed me with seedlings
and fruit.

I returned clothed
in grapes and grain.

I brought back the seed
of straightforward schools,
foliage steeled
by new-built factories,
the heartbeat
of tenacity and the movement
of growth peopling itself
with fragrance.

In one place
I saw bread diminished
while farther on
kingdoms of sheaves

extend themselves.

I saw in the villages war
like discarded
teeth
and I saw elsewhere
the circle of peace
growing like a goblet,
like a child in the womb.

I have seen.

Where I was,
even
among the thorns
that sought to harm me,
I found that a dove
in its flight was stitching
my heart to other
hearts.
I found in all places
bread, wine, fire, hands,
tenderness.

I slept beneath all
the flags
united
as under the branches
of a single green forest
and the stars were
my stars.

From my cruel battles,
from my sorrows,
I hold onto nothing
that would not serve you.

And also like the land,
I belong to all.
Not a single drop
of hate remains in my breast.
My hands are open
casting grapes
to the wind.

I returned from my journeys.
I journeyed
building joy.

Let love defend us.

Let the rose
lift up
her new garments.
Let the florid land
be endlessly flowering.

Between the mountains
and the snow-white waves
of Chile,
reborn in the blood
of my people,
for all of you,
for you I sing.

Let all song be shared
throughout the world.

Let the grape vines arise.
Let the wind spread them about.

Let it be so.

Translator's Afterword and Acknowledgements

I first became acquainted with *Las Uvas y el Viento* while a high school exchange student in Santiago, Chile during the very open and liberal democratic era just prior to the election of Salvador Allende. The school I attended, Liceo Manuel de Salas, was an experimental school run and largely staffed by faculty of the University of Chile. As a going-away present, I was given an illustrated copy of the poem's central section, *Cuando de Chile/When, Chile*, and have kept it as a valued memento ever since. Several years ago, having left the practice of law and taken the opportunity to free up my time for other interests, I looked for a copy of the much longer poem of which that section is a part. While Spanish is my second language and I therefore was happy to find the original 1954 Spanish edition, as published in Argentina, I was also surprised to discover that the work had apparently never been translated into English in whole or in part. Instead, from all that appeared, it had only been translated into German, Romanian and Hungarian, and then not since the mid-1950's.

I contacted the Neruda Estate's literary agent, the late Carmen Balcells, and she confirmed that for whatever reason, the poem had escaped translation or much notice during the poet's lifetime, and none since. She also confirmed the Estate's interest in seeing the work reach a larger public. I therefore began the gradual process leading to this translation and am now pleased to offer it to an English readership.

One might speculate that with its several encomia to such discredited dictators as Lenin, Stalin and Mao the poem might well have seemed an unlikely money-maker to Western European or US publishers when it first appeared in 1954. And the few translations made at the time were in fact limited to a handful of minor Soviet satellite countries–East Germany, Romania and Hungary–and none followed anywhere else. As Helene de Aguilar correctly observes in her accompanying essay, it's clear that some portions of the work are weakened to the extent they seek to convey a blunt political message in less than poetic form. But she is also right, now that we are more than 60 years on from the moment, that the poem as a whole takes on what was, given Neruda's epic skills, quite likely an independently mythic construct of leaders, countries and citizens in their universally idealized form – *i.e.*, as they might have been free of their necessary temporality.

In my reading, the poem as a whole is also more broadly a love song to his native land written from afar during his wandering exile. I found the greatest part of this lengthy work reflective of the imaginative lyricism that marks Neruda at his best – verses filled with passionate, creative and unexpected imagery. And given that the poem dates from the mature period of his *Canto General* and *Odas Elementales*, that should be no surprise.

To the question how to translate Neruda in a way that is both faithful to the Spanish and still poetic in English, I can only give a personal answer. I adhered wherever possible to the formal structure of the poem – preserving Neruda's line breaks and other constructions, for example. More generally, I kept to simple, concrete English words consistent with Neruda's use of the same in Spanish. "Earthy" is certainly one apt description of his imagery, reliant as it is on trees, plants, soil, metal, stone and wood. He often uses the same Spanish word for these elements but in widely varied contexts – I mostly did the same.

I also avoided obscure vocabulary as best I could, instead trying to maintain the directness of speech that characterizes much of Neruda's poetry, and certainly characterizes this poem. It is of course true that Neruda can be notoriously hermetic and there are some images, some verses, that defy easy explanation. I therefore simply tried to play them as they lay. If they are hard to understand in English, all I can say is that the secret may forever remain locked in the poetic moment. By and large, however, I aimed for language that might as easily be spoken as written – colloquial, conversational and personal.

Let me close by expressing my deep gratitude to Helene de Aguilar not only for bringing her keen scholarship to bear in the thoughtful introduction she has written to the poem, but also for the editorial suggestions (and improvements) she made on early drafts of the work. I likewise am grateful to my daughter Pippa Straus, who added her own skillful editing hand to refinement of the final product. It has also been a pleasure to work with Agencia Literaria Carmen Balcells. And finally to my patient and tolerant wife Philippa and my always supportive son Marc – thank you for bearing with me and allowing the space and time I've dedicated to this project.

Michael Straus

Biographical Notes

Pablo Neruda was the pen name of the Chilean poet, diplomat and politician Ricardo Reyes Basoalto (1904-73). Writing in a variety of modes including love poems and other lyrics, historical epics, political manifestos and a prose autobiography, Neruda won the Nobel Prize for Literature in 1971. He was justly called "the greatest poet of the 20th century in any language" by the Colombia novelist and fellow Nobel Prize winner Gabriel García Marquez.

Michael Straus first became acquainted with Neruda's poetry while in high school as an exchange student in Santiago, Chile. Fluent in Spanish, he also holds graduate degrees in law and classical languages.

Dr. Helene Jf de Aguilar holds a Masters Degree in Latin-American history from NYU and a Doctorate in literature from Columbia University. A recipient of a Columbia University Faculty Fellowship, a Mellon Grant, a Woodrow Wilson Fellowship and a Fulbright Fellowship she taught a wide variety of courses, principally at Barnard College and at Columbia University, over the course of some 37 years. She has been a frequent contributor to *Parnassus: Poetry in Review*.

Anna Pipes is an artist and illustrator living and working in New York City. She creates paintings, drawings, prints and collages that explore fantasy, illusion and mystery. She loves the way visual art can communicate incongruities and impossibilities.